NEW YORK Central

AND THE

TRAINS

of the Future

by

Geoffrey H. Doughty

TLC
PUBLISHING INC.

1997
TLC Publishing Inc.
1387 Winding Creek Lane
Lynchburg, Virginia • 24503-3776

Front Cover Illustration: The dawning of a new era in rail passenger service was hoped for in many places in the mid 1950s, but the technology of the *Xplorer, Aerotrain* and others was not fully developed in time to save a rapidly dying industry. Artwork by Kenneth L. Miller based on an original photograph by John S. Gallagher.

End Sheet: J. Parker Lamb caught the *Xplorer* racing northbound through the farmland north of Fairborn, Ohio (15 miles north of Dayton) on a fine spring day in 1957.

Back Cover Illustration: This painting by noted rail artist Andrew Harmantas depicts the high expectations and hopes that New York Central's leadership had for its Train of the Future. Unfortunately for its designers and its chief promoter, dark clouds were the horizon and the train and passenger service's future was not as bright as it might have been.

Dedication

New York Central & the Trains of the Future is dedicated to the memory of
John deNervaud Wolf
my friend and colleague, who was intrigued by and understood anything mechanical. His talents, sense of humor, and sense of perspective are greatly missed by those who knew him.

Library of Congress Catalog Number 97-60352
ISBN 1-883089-28-X

Layout and Design by
Kenneth L. Miller, Miller Design & Photography, Salem, Virginia

Printed by
Walsworth Publishing
Marceline Missouri

Contents

"It has long been recognized in the transport industry that vehicle design and performance have a powerful and pervasive influence over the investment requirements, operating and maintenance costs, and the traffic and revenue generating capabilities of all transport services."

Alan R. Cripe, 1924-1994

"We must test these trains critically, but only with the idea of taking back to the manufacturers information which will enable them to improve their next models, and the ones after that."

Robert R. Young, chairman of NYC
as quoted in *Railway Age*, May 7, 1956

Acknowledgements

"From the outset it was apparent that it is impossible, under present-day competitive conditions, to produce revenues capable of sustaining present costs. It follows, therefore, that the creation of a profitable passenger operation must necessarily be based on a service which can be produced at substantially lower costs."

Quoted from an internal NYC memo dated September 24, 1958 regarding the subject of long-range passenger service plans.

New *York Central & the Trains of the Future* is as much a story about the fate of America's passenger trains as it is about the experimentals which were supposed to rescue them from oblivion. It is a story which could not have been told without the invaluable help of persons who were familiar with their creation and operation over their short lifespan, and who documented their passing into, through, and from the railroad scene.

First and foremost, this story could not have been told without the thoughtful advice, guidance, and recollections of John S. Gallagher, Jr., NYC's director of passenger research, and W. D. Edson, NYC's chief mechanical engineer, both of whom recounted for me the reasons behind *Xplorer's* creation and the decisions which were being made behind the facade of NYC's optimistic promotions of the times and who took time to review the text. Their insight into the train's failures and successes has been illuminating and the story is richer as a result. Each spent considerable amounts of time editing and pointing me in various directions to pursue different issues which played a part in the story of the trains and the railroads of the period. I am deeply indebted to each for his generous time and interest - not to mention patience.

Theodore Shrady and Richard Sprague also reviewed the text and made suggestions for its improvement. Their time and consideration, as well as perspective, are also greatly appreciated.

A faithful few who have contributed to my previous accounts of NYC's passenger operations have again lent photographs of the period which have helped tell this tale. Among them are Victor Baird, Robert Hadley, Herb Harwood, David Randall, J. W. Swanberg, H. Lans Vail, Jr., and Jay Williams. These are the custodians of historic photographs which, when taken, were mere tokens of interest

Harold K. Vollrath Collection
The Boston and Maine/Maine Central *Flying Yankee* was similar in concept and design to the Burlington's *Zephyrs*.

Jay Williams Collection
One of streamlining's most famous manifestations was the 1941 *Empire State Express* seen en route to Buffalo a few days after its inaugural on December 7, 1941.

without thought to their future importance. I am indebted to each for his interest, time and generosity, as they have become important sources of information.

I am especially grateful to William Vantuono of Simmons-Boardman Publishing Company for permission to reprint excerpts from the *Railway Age* archives. The magazines proved to be a storehouse of information which accurately documented this important period of railroad history.

A retired Big Four engineer, "Brownie" Markley, wrote me one day during this book's preparation and in subsequent correspondence related stories about the *Xplorer,* one of which is reprinted herein. I am grateful for his contribution and knowledge of his first-hand experiences.

My publisher, Tom Dixon, unearthed a wealth of information from his vaults and files which furthered my research and allowed me a broader perspective of the projects. His foresight in their collection only goes to prove that there are some things that one should never throw out, no matter how unimportant they may seem at the time.

Andrew Harmantas and I collaborated on the rear cover painting of the *Xplorer* passing Berea. By the time the train was in service, the station had actually fallen victim to lack of maintenance and the effects of Mother Nature. But with the exercise of artistic license, Berea has stood well the eroding elements of time. Working with him has been a most enjoyable pleasure.

Another enjoyable working relationship has been with layout artist Ken Miller. He shares an affection for the subject matter and has a flair for presenting the drama inherent in railroading.

My computer guru who lives for train books, Wanda Worrey, has again excelled where others have feared to trespass. She is an experienced hand at composition and without her I would have had great difficulty in this book's publication. I am indebted to her and fortunate that she is so forgiving.

My wife, Pamela, has also been forgiving of her husband's preoccupation with this book, not to mention her ignoring the clutter which has liberally littered the living room. Her tolerance has been pushed to the limits presently known to mankind, and I only wish there were some way to make it up to her. She and the dogs have learned to step around piles of photographs and step over files of correspondence, all of which has made me especially grateful.

This book, then, is not unlike the trains—made from the works of many suppliers. To each and every one I am grateful for their contributions beyond the borders of my expression.

Streamlining was considered to be a "wave of the future" when it was combined with Art Deco styling, especially where railroad passenger equipment was concerned. Passengers (who apparently didn't wipe their feet before entering the car) became accustomed to elegant passenger accommodations and comforts such as on the 1938 *20th Century Limited's* observation car lounge.

Preface

As this is being written, we are witnessing the 40th anniversary of the signing of the Interstate Highway Act on June 29, 1956 by President Dwight D. Eisenhower. He signed this piece of legislation with the hope that the billions of dollars to be spent on the proposed 45,000-mile interstate highway system would be a wise investment for America's future. Most of the money was used for highway construction, with little thought given to the cost of maintenance or its consequence upon the privately financed, tax paying railroads. Between 1956 and 1995, for example, the Interstate Highway Fund spent 307 billion dollars on the nation's highways. In 1993 alone, federal, state, and local governments combined spent 88.5 billion dollars on highway construction and maintenance.

Eisenhower prophesied that the construction of the network would aid in this country's defense, promote interstate commerce, and bind together the cities and towns along its many routes — much in the same way as the railroads had for generations. Support industries would be created and existing services would expand, creating employment opportunities for all Americans.

The interstate highway system represented the future of America, he said. It was a noble mission and one whose benefits were to manifest themselves much in the way that Eisenhower envisioned. It also established a deeply-rooted national transportation policy which, as one of its unintended side effects, was to damage the viability of the railroad industry—especially in the industrialized and densely populated northeast.

So while the Act spelled out a future for industry and future employment, the nation's railroads were struggling to find ways to secure their futures. Fifteen years after the Act's signing, Amtrak would be created to salvage the passenger train, and five years after that, Conrail would be formed from the remains of six northeast bankrupt railroads to salvage and restore the region's rail network.

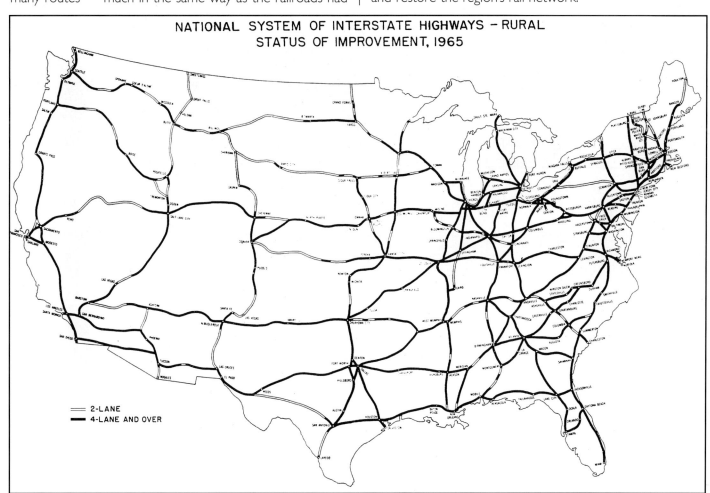

U.S. Bureau of Public Roads - 1955

The Interstate Highway Act of 1956 provided for a network of federally funded interstate highways which would reach from coast to coast by 1965.

Today, many simplistically blame only the interstate highways and the airlines for the passenger train's demise. Indeed, both played a role, but were it not for a government policy which encouraged their development as early as 1916, in the case of the U.S. Highway network, and 1946 with the Federal Airport Act, which laid the foundation for future expenditures on airport projects, and the railroads themselves, the demise might have been more gradual—but just as important, not necessarily prevented.

During the course of writing my first two books about New York Central Railroad's great passenger train fleet in the postwar era, I was constantly reminded of the role that one man played in the railroad industry at the time and the efforts he made to save the dying passenger train industry with the development of "new trains." His name was Robert R. Young, and his innovations, not to mention the controversy he generated, coupled with his most notable "failure," called *Xplorer*, seemed to pop up time and time again. As they did, so did the year 1956 - and it became clear that there was more of a story to be told which extended beyond what is generally thought of the man, the train, the period, and New York Central's "Great Steel Fleet." And as quickly as *Xplorer* and its General Motors' counterpart, *Aerotrain*, burst onto the public stage, they quietly disappeared.

What makes this so interesting is that all of the efforts of the industry to produce a new train concept coalesced in 1956, making it the year that could have been the turning point for the passenger train industry. And by the end of 1956 (!), the railroads and the press suddenly became silent on the subject of "new trains."

Today, *Xplorer* and *Aerotrain* are mostly remembered for their rough rides. In a sense this is an injustice. Their rides were rough, but the trains were experimental and given time their suspensions might have been improved. It didn't take long to realize that few knew the real story behind their creation and with what enthusiasm their creators took on the challenge of their work. Even at the time of their debut many derided the trains, and so few really understood the complexity of what they were intended to accomplish. Even less was understood about Robert Young, and upon the trains' failure, many heaped scorn on what was believed to be Young's folly.

Many regarded Young as a pariah, or worse, a power-hungry egomaniac. Some viewed him as a maverick; some as a populist; and a few saw him as a visionary. In turn, Young saw those who disagreed with him as out of step with the times. Regardless of what many thought of him, and still think of him today, he was an important advocate of the industry. That people still talk of him today is an indication of his widespread influence.

The New York Central Railroad (NYC) is probably best remembered for its famous *20th Century Limited* and the parade of passenger trains which were a part of its *Great Steel Fleet*. Perhaps not as well known is that it also went through a phase of innovation in the last 18 years of its corporate identity which earned it a reputation within the industry as a pioneer in both passenger and freight transportation. In large part, this was due to the efforts of Robert R. Young.

As prolific as were NYC's operations, its financial health was anything but robust following World War II. The reasons for this condition do not concern us here, but the health of the rail industry as a whole (and the passenger train) in the early to mid-1950s does play a part in telling the story about the lightweight train experiments of the period, and in particular, about what started out as *Train X*, and its descendants—NYC's *Xplorer*, and General Motors' *Aerotrain*.

In some respects, *Train X* was not unlike Burlington's *Zephyr*, Illinois Central's *Green Diamond*, the New Haven's *Comet* and Union Pacific's *M-10000* of 15 years before. They were designed to address specific engineering and marketing objectives within the parameters of an experimental concept, and were predicated upon changing the industry's perception and application of basic engineering principles, while making more productive use of labor. *Train X*, therefore, has to be placed in an historical context because its underlying concept embodied the experience gained from these earlier experiments, combined with an attempt to reduce the influence of the institutional, political and economical issues involved. In other words, it tried to address all that was wrong with the passenger train and make it all that it should have been. Although almost everyone knows that these trains fell short of their goals, we must look at the forces which defeated them in order to fully comprehend their failures—and appreciate how they altered the future course of the industry.

Improved Schedule For The
CINCINNATI MERCURY

between

**CINCINNATI,
MIDDLETOWN,
DAYTON,
SPRINGFIELD,
COLUMBUS,
CLEVELAND**

Northbound: Earlier departure from Cincinnati — mid-evening arrival in Cleveland.

Southbound: A pleasant morning trip from Cleveland.

Coaches, parlor and parlor observation cars. Refreshment lounge and dining car for all passengers. See Time Table 22, above, for schedule details.

For Pullman, Coach and Dining Car Service, see Pages 6

The *Green Diamond* was Illinois Central's entry into the world of streamlined articulated trains.

And, actually, there was more than one *Train X*. From the drafting tables of the progressive mechanical design engineer Alan Cripe of the Chesapeake and Ohio Railway came initial designs; then a *Train X* test coach designed and built in collaboration with Pullman-Standard, the leading passenger car manufacturer of the era. Between 1951 and 1955 further refinements were made before pursuit of "new trains" began in earnest on a broader scale, and as might be expected, the *Xplorer* of 1956 was a different vehicle than that which was envisioned ten years earlier.

The story of *Xplorer* and *Aerotrain* is a complex tale about NYC's transition from the road of the *Great Steel Fleet* to the "Road to the Future," which begins in the corporate offices of the Chesapeake & Ohio Railway and in particular, the office occupied by its chairman, Robert R. Young. The two trains, the two railroads, and the highly controversial R. R. Young are all interconnected, and to discuss one without discussing the others would not give the reader a complete picture in the context of the times. To complicate matters further, there is the intriguing story about the motives for the trains' development; the interest groups involved, which included the railroad unions and the financial community; the role of government; and the various conflicts between the realists and the idealists, all of which determined the experimentals' destiny. And interwoven with the story of *Xplorer* is the story of what happened to NYC's passenger operations; and by extension, what happened to the American passenger train. So, there is a story within the story—a 3-D snapshot of the period.

Because of this complexity, I have begun with an overview in order to lay the foundation for what follows. This may help the reader to sort out the details.

In an article titled "Who Shot the Passenger Train?" (TRAINS Magazine, April 1959), the late David P. Morgan contended that there was not one single assassin, but a firing squad. The train was not killed, however. It was shot and wounded by a combination of people, events, and circumstances. While its health improved with governmental intravenous feeding, it still had fatal weaknesses which have imperiled its stability since Amtrak's inception—namely, the lack of significant numbers of riders to cover expenses, and the shift in the passenger train's role from a revenue provider under private operation to that of a service provider under the auspices of government, subject to the caprice of politicians.

Meanwhile, air passenger transport today is operating at full capacity. It is held hostage daily to the threat of terrorism; it has rapidly degenerated into a "take it or leave it" service, complete with surly attendants, discourteous ticket counter representatives, uncomfortable seats, peanuts instead of meals, and the inconvenience of delays and cancellations without explanation, mostly for the convenience of the airline. Quite often, one's baggage earns more frequent flyer-miles than its owner; and even the safety of air flight operations is being called into question.

And back on earth, our highways are still clogged with traffic. So, America still needs its passenger trains - although our political leaders who control Amtrak's destiny may not realize it.

I have written *New York Central and the Trains of the Future* as a companion volume to *New York Central's Great Steel Fleet* (published by TLC in 1995) because this chapter of that railroad's history held such significant implications for the course of America's passenger trains. It turned out that NYC was in the lead in trying to solve the "passenger problem." In fact, one cannot fully appreciate the future of today's rail passenger network without a look at the experiments which NYC and others made in the attempt to compensate for the passenger train's inherent flaws. *Xplorer* and *Aerotrain* are relevant today because their development laid out the map to where passenger rail transport should be headed.

While the appearance and role of the passenger train have changed, many of the problems for which NYC sought solutions have remained. Circumstances prevented the railroad from further exploration for answers to the passenger dilemma in 1956—a dilemma which still today many believe cannot be resolved. Perhaps some day an impartial paladin of history will record that it was this conviction alone which became the single largest obstacle to NYC and the trains of the future.

Geoffrey H. Doughty
January 1997

An early (1948) artist's conception of *Train X* shows the train curving through one of many river valleys along the C&O's right of way. The locomotive is similar in design to GM's *Aerotrain* design of ten years later.

Troubled Times - 1946-1956

At the midpoint of the 20th century, New York Central was second only to the Pennsylvania Railroad in passenger traffic volume. It operated a vast passenger service fleet, including commuter trains in Boston, New York, Detroit, and Chicago, and some of the most famous intercity trains in the world. Following the end of World War II, however, the fleet's base of support was being undermined by several forces—regulations, organized labor, and transportation's "progress."

NYC faced serious challenges in the postwar period, many of which were still on its agenda at war's end, and others which were to catch its management by surprise. These challenges would dramatically alter the course of NYC's viability and the future course of the railroad industry. Both freight and passenger traffic, which had expanded during the war, fell steadily after its conclusion. Still, the railroad moved boldly in reorganizing and restructuring its facilities and services—and ordering new passenger equipment thinking that these would help it recapture and, ultimately, sustain a healthy passenger traffic operation.

America's railroads realized that passenger traffic was moving away from them to other modes, but it was a move which they were slow to recognize. In fact, it seems they were incapable of reacting and adjusting to the new preferences of the public. This was the historic nature of the railroad industry, mired in tradition and meeting new situations head-on with old solutions. Nevertheless, there were individuals within the industry, while few in number, who saw the need for imagination and creativity in seeking solutions to its woes.

Meanwhile, along with other of America's railroads, NYC was struggling with the passenger train dilemma. Facing declining revenues in both its freight and passenger operations, it needed creative solutions—something out of character for the conservative and stoic NYC management. Compounding its problems, the railroad was hampered by existing public regulations which limited its ability to eliminate unprofitable services, set rates, and earn a profit; and union contracts which impeded efficient use of personnel. Indeed, management seemed stunned and incapable.

The postwar American passenger train began encountering deep trouble as early as 1950. It soon became apparent that the millions of dollars which NYC and other railroads had spent on new passenger equipment and service improvements following World War II had been squandered as Americans abandoned the rails in favor of the independence of the automobile and time-saving of the airplane. The public was aided in their new preferences by government policies which expended billions of tax dollars on interstate highways, large commercial airport projects, and on the automotive and aviation equipment industries.

The American public has always been fascinated by anything new and often what has captured attention was its preoccupation with new modes of passenger transport. There was a time when passenger transport meant trains and luxury liners and it was hoped that the recently re-equipped trains would draw the interest of the public back to the rails. Unfortunately, while the railroads were ordering new and shiny streamlined passenger equipment for their fleets, they ignored the need to change the economics of their operations.

Of course, the hopes of the industry were misguided. The public did not respond as the railroads had expected and it wasn't long before there was talk of "new trains"—trains of the future—and NYC would be a leader in their promotion. Initially, however, NYC did not figure so prominently in the development of these trains. It was only through the twists of corporate fortune that the company ultimately fulfilled the ambition of the man who had invested so much of his own personal wealth, time and energy for its control.

In many respects, the meteoric rise in interest with the trains of the future was the result of one man's vision—and passion. In the person of Robert R. Young, the passenger train's most vocal supporter, the rail traveler had a charismatic and indefatigable champion.

Born in Texas on February 14, 1897, Young was the rebellious son a of a local Texas banker. After the death of his mother, his father, completely at a loss as to what to do with his recalcitrant son, sent young Robert to an orphanage. When he was old enough, he was sent to attend Culver Military Academy, from where he went on to attend the University of Virginia for a year - before dropping out.

At 18, he married Anita O'Keefe, the younger sister of artist Georgia O'Keefe. Young went to work for du Pont Corporation in an ammunition plant and worked his way up to the treasurer's office where he employed his talents garnered from a two-year correspondence course in business administration. At the same time he learned the principles of advertising and how to enlist public opinion. These courses, combined with his innate flair for business, his voracious desire to succeed at everything he tried, and his flamboyant nature, would serve him well in the years ahead when he would employ them to the disadvantage of his opponents.

He began his rise as a financial advisor at General Motors (GM) in the mid-1920s. Young left GM in 1928 and amassed a personal fortune in the stock market at the onset of the Depression. He became disenchanted with the manner in which the small investor always seemed to be shortchanged by those who controlled big business. Soon, his cause became the interests of what was then known as "the little guy"—the investors who owned 100-500 shares of stock. As a result, some have called him a "populist."

By 1942, Robert R. Young was the uninhibited chairman of the board of the Chesapeake & Ohio (C&O) and its parent, Alleghany Corporation. Alleghany* was a holding company which controlled several railroads, which included, at one time or another (in addition to C&O),

C&O Historical Society

Robert R. Young, 1897-1958

the conveyance of choice and return profits for its owners. Young believed that while the traveler might be lured away from rail travel, he could be persuaded to return. This would require a train of a totally new design to fit the needs of the traveling public, however. More importantly, the railroad industry would have to change the way it conducted business if it were to survive in the postwar era.

The vision Young had for a train of new design was a lightweight, low center of gravity, high-speed train which could operate over the existing railbeds of America. He called it "Train X," for lack of a better name. Developed when Young was at C&O, the coal hauler wasn't the right place for it. C&O's passenger base and right-of-way just weren't suited for the train Young envisioned.

Then, in December 1946, NYC became the focus of a takeover bid by Robert R. Young—the first of two such attempts. Believing that NYC wielded immense power and influence in the financial world, as well as within the railroad boardrooms of America, Young saw that his best chance for instituting change within the industry was being in control

the Erie, the Missouri Pacific, the Nickel Plate, the Pere Marquette, and the Wheeling and Lake Erie. Through Alleghany, Young sought to influence the course of the railroad industry which led him to locked combat with the established railroad order, its governmental regulators, and the Wall Street investment houses, all of whom Young perceived as inimical to change and who controlled industry for their own selfish gain.

As far as the railroads' passenger services were concerned, Young felt that it was how rail passenger transport was produced and marketed and how it was mired in traditional trappings and customs that was dragging it down the road to oblivion. If only the train and its managers could be freed of the bonds of traditionalism, government over-regulation and outdated union work rules, the passenger train could once again be

of NYC. Initially Young would be rebuffed, but he would continue his battle to control the company, and years later conducted an unprecedented publicity campaign through the newsprint media, while occasionally appearing on the newest medium, television. Young was in his element in this confrontation with the Wall Street titans, and the ferocity of the campaign took his opponents by surprise.

Beset by declining traffic, NYC faced bankruptcy in 1954. It would be avoided by Young, who in that year won control of the railroad through a protracted and often bitter proxy battle. It emerged from this battle a very different company. Paired with a new president, Alfred Perlman, Young would transform NYC so that it could assume the mantle of a progressive leader of the railroad industry.

Passenger service, the object of Young's attention, continued in decline—not just on NYC, but across the spectrum of America's railroads. It was a decline which had its origins in the Depression, with a respite during World War II, only to

*Legend has it that the corporation was named after the Allegheny Mountains, but that Allegheny was misspelled in the legal documents and it was not noticed until after the incorporation papers were approved—in actuality, Alleghany is the local Virginia spelling, but the pronunciation is the same.

resume following the conflict. The decline continued to push the long-distance passenger train to the point of extinction. In the meantime, while NYC was modernizing its operations, Young rolled out his train of the future (*Train X*), renamed *Xplorer,* to "solve" the passenger problem—although he realized that the changes which were occurring in society's travel habits were well beyond amelioration merely by the innovations he envisioned.

In late 1956, the country entered into a deep recession, and in 1957, the railroad industry faced its worst year since the war. It couldn't have happened at a worse time. With shrinking freight traffic and revenues, NYC's passenger deficits, which had hovered between $30 and $55 million a year since 1947, were a burden that could no longer be sustained by the railroad in light of the recession. This added urgency to Young's ideas and plans—and complicated them. Success in his endeavors would elude him.

Was Young sincere in his motives or was he simply an opportunist? Perhaps an in-depth look at Robert R. Young could best answer this question, but in the meantime, one can imagine that it might be both. Perhaps "pragmatist" is more accurate. It doesn't really matter, for he championed a cause which others in the industry were all too willing to abandon and when given the opportunity to enact his theories, he seized it.

Of course, he rarely moved in only one direction at a time. This explains why he took on the industry, its unions, and the government simultaneously. It was quite characteristic for him to be espousing diverse innovations, policies and services concurrently. He attacked on all fronts. And what the public saw were his pronouncements as reported in the press. What they failed to do was examine and understand Young's motives to improve passenger train service, which seemed to get lost in the rhetoric.

Young was a renegade investment banker who believed that "capitalism had to be saved from the capitalists" who corrupted the free market process.[1] Although he was hardly angelic, his motives were driven by a peculiar sense of societal (capitalistic) altruism - every investor had a right to benefit from his investments. He was at his best when on the offensive and would take his opponents by surprise utilizing as one of his chief weapons his uncanny talent for marshaling public opinion. While being charming and gracious, he could be scheming and calculating. His primary goal was to change existing regulations and loosen the grip on the throat of the railroads of the banking interests, the union establishment, and public regulators, so that the railroads could earn more money. He believed that the banking and union interests exercised excessive influence over the railroads which prevented the industry from managing their operations with greater flexibility and earning greater profits.

Combating the banking interests was particularly vexing. The banks controlled the capital the railroad needed for

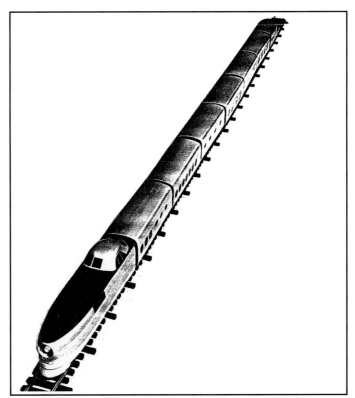

C&O Historical Society

A model of *Train X* was developed utilizing the anticipated styling for the locomotive and ACF Talgo coaches.

improvements—from new locomotives to the physical plant. They expected a return on their investments—in other words, they were accustomed to taking more money out of the railroads than they put into them. They saw innovation—particularly passenger service innovation—as too risky, since there was little hope of making any profit. Their other transportation interests, mainly the growing airline and automotive industries - with their strong government backing - were far more promising investments. Here Young would have to employ his considerable skills and talents as a manipulator.

As far as the unions were concerned, they were opposed to any change in working conditions which would result in improved operating efficiency, since this would mean the loss of union jobs or a reduction in pay for their members - and a reduction in union influence. The brotherhoods, supported by other unions, had considerable political clout with elected officials, at all levels, which was exercised anytime the railroad petitioned regulatory agencies to remove passenger trains or make changes in service. Train and engine crews would not be the only ones affected by such changes, however, but so would maintenance personnel, station personnel, switching crews, etc.

The infamous state "full crew" laws were kept intact decades after technological improvements and advancement in communications made traditional staffing of passenger trains unnecessary. Such measures inflated already costly passenger train operations at a time when some states mandated the operation of passenger trains in the public interest, even when there was little or no demand for the service they provided.

In order to effect change, Young needed to combat the forces opposed to change, and to accomplish this he would need a powerful ally. He had an ambitious plan.

Young saw passenger service (i.e. the passenger train and *Train X*) as a means to an end. Because the banks and the unions were so politically influential, diminishing the influence of railroad management, he realized that he needed to galvanize the support of America's most politically potent interest group—the voting public—to attain his goals. To accomplish this, he attached himself to a cause which he believed affected them on the broadest scale—how they traveled. Improving passenger train service became his crusade. This mission would figure prominently in his fight for the Pullman Company, and soon after that, New York Central.

Up to the mid-1940s, most of America traveled by rail. Railroads ran all across America, reaching almost every city and town, giving almost every citizen some contacts with the railroad. They had a relative who was employed by the railroad, or knew someone who worked for it. They put pennies on tracks as children; passenger trains took them off to camp in the summer; and to towns and cities to visit relatives. When business required travel—it was by rail. By 1950, however, the very manner in which people were conveyed was in transition, and this fact alone would undermine Young's efforts.

Even at that early date, the Pullman Company was concerned enough to commission a report about its future. Prepared by Robert Heller and Associates of Cleveland, the consulting firm came to some startling conclusions when it delivered the report beginning in August 1951. Utilizing data from the Interstate Commerce Commission, the Civil Aeronautics Board, the Air Transport Association, the Association of American Railroads, and several railroads, the report stated that "airline passenger-miles increased from 85 million in 1930 to 8,133 million in 1950, whereas Pullman decreased from 12,515 million to 9,174 million. There is a strong basic natural demand for Pullman transportation … but railroad and Pullman service is generally unsatisfactory in light of competitive conditions."[2]

The report held the railroads responsible for the decline in traffic and cited the results of its passenger surveys which found passenger dissatisfaction with rough rides, old equipment, trains operating at such fast speeds precluding the chance to get a good night's sleep, and perhaps the fatal blow, that "railroads in general give Pullman passengers the impression that they do not want their business."[3] It continued by adding that the railroads were not being effective in their marketing attempts and that there was much room for improvement. The report was delivered to Pullman and not made public.

Unfortunately for Young, the attention and interest of the public in the fate of the passenger train was evaporating. In addition, few within the industry had any interest or faith in Young's innovations. At a time when the industry was struggling (with little success) in their attempts to abandon passenger service, here was Young exclaiming publicly that the railroads had mostly themselves to blame for their crisis. His criticism was about as welcome as mosquitoes at an outdoor barbecue. Nevertheless, while he was sometimes feared, often mistrusted, and cautiously respected, Young became the influential driving force of change.

Caught in a 3-way squeeze between government regulation, a hostile financial community and the union lobby, and the limitations of existing technology and private capital, Young knew the difficulties ahead of him were formidable. There was little or nothing he could do about the former, and restrictions were imposed on what he could do about the latter. Still, he proceeded, and made a lot of noise in the process to draw attention to himself and his causes.

And what attention he generated! As far as the press was concerned, they knew that Young always made good copy. The flamboyant nature of his approach usually placed him on the front pages of many newspapers, and in the process, Robert R. Young became a "household" name. Through speeches, articles, and his constant battle with the railroads and its regulators, which he fought in the courts, the hearing rooms of Congress, as well as in the press, the railroad industry was ultimately persuaded, albeit reluctantly, to join him in his crusade for the train of the future.

Very soon, new trains and passenger cars were rolling off the drawing boards and the assembly track. In 1955 and 1956, with the Korean War recently off the front pages of America's newspapers, innovation in passenger transport once again was capturing the public's attention—but not for long.

All the publicity and all the optimistic forecasts could not overcome the trains' lack of public appeal, however. While being promoted as only experimental, the public's response was unenthusiastic. The trains were viewed by many, both inside and outside the industry, as duds.

Were these trains aberrations of a select few who should have known better? Certainly not. They were sincere but belated attempts to change the course of rail passenger transport to coincide with the changes in the markets they were intended to serve. That they fell short of their goals does not mean that the goals were illusions, or simply elusive. If they were the latter, it was only for a brief period. In fact, many of the passenger service theories which lay at the foundation of *Xplorer* are being practiced today by Amtrak, and its Canadian and European counterparts. And today's Amtrak, Metro-North, Metra, and New Jersey Transit—to name but a few—were outgrowths of NYC's passenger studies of the mid-1950s.

In 1956 and 1957, however, the financial community and

One of the streamlined Hudson locomotives styled for use on the *Empire State Express* of 1941 has a new nameplate on its front for use on its new assignment, the westbound *Chicago Mercury,* seen at Dearborn, Michigan circa 1950.

the railroads were in no condition to invest in the new trains with so little hope for a return on their investment. Furthermore, the railroads were poised to abandon passenger service while the public was all too easily lured to the convenience of the other modes of travel available to them. The experimental trains became the trains of the future, but in concept only—the country just wasn't ready for them.

At the time they made their debut, *Xplorer* and the *Aerotrain* were thought by some to be the industry's salvation. Ten years later they were all but forgotten—and so

were America's passenger trains. For a brief time, however, NYC and the trains of the future occupied center stage. Their promoter turned out to be ahead of his time (for many of the other innovations he championed came to fruition)—a time when creativity and imagination were barely alive in the boardrooms of America's railroads—and only a few had the courage and the means to set their bold ideas into motion.

The New York Central opens a new era in rail transportation with this fabulous new "dream train"

THIS TRAIN WILL SAVE AN INDUSTRY

The New York Central brings you a fast, lightweight new train that can revolutionize rail travel, increase employment, and strengthen our national defense.

This new "dream train" is like nothing you've ever seen before—and it will soon be rolling on the New York Central.

Designed and built by General Motors, it makes a clean break with the past. Like today's Chevrolet compared with the old high wheelers, it is lighter, lower, faster and much quieter and more comfortable —all at much lower cost.

But the most important thing about this train is that it can actually save America's railroad passenger business.

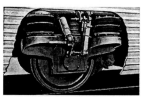

Cars are literally suspended on air—Air under pressure fills the doughnut like rubber bellows at each end of the wheel truck. Vibration and noise are absorbed passing through the air . . . giving the smoothest, most comfortable ride you've ever felt.

Few of those who sometimes justifiably criticize railroad passenger service realize that the cost of building and operating present high wheel equipment has become so prohibitive that the railroads lost almost 700 *million* dollars on this service during the last year.

The railroads are up against subsidized competition from airlines, busses, and private automobiles—to say nothing of restrictions imposed by regulatory bodies, so often politically motivated.

These factors combine to make it impossible for us to set fares which can even come close to making up our loss. Last year this passenger loss nearly equalled the total net income that America's railroads earned from *all* sources.

We know of no other industry required to render service at a loss. Not even the strongest one can do so long, even if public opinion or our Constitution would permit it.

Needless to say, this is a very serious

situation—from the railroads' standpoint and from the public's. And it's even more serious from the standpoint of national defense. To keep our country strong, we need strong, vigorous, up-to-date railroads.

Trains like the one you see above can convert the present shrinking railroad passenger industry into a dynamic, growing one. With a steel underframe and aluminum body, it is 50% lighter than standard trains. *It is 60% less expensive to build and 60% less expensive to operate.*

It will enable us to offer faster, smoother service—and to keep passenger fares at a lower level than they otherwise must be. And by revitalizing the railroad business, it can lead to more employment.

The train pictured here is the first of *two* "dream trains" soon to be running on the Central. The second, called "Train X," is now being built by Pullman-Standard. The Central is doing all it can to encourage these two manufacturers to quickly go into volume production of these new trains.

We salute General Motors for building our first new train. Next Spring it will go into service between Chicago and Detroit in a speedy daylight run. When you look it over, see if you don't agree that a new era in railroading has begun.

New York Central Railroad

Collection of Wm. D. Edson

In late 1954, in anticipation of *Aerotrain's* delivery, NYC published this advertisement which set out the railroad's argument about its passenger train losses - for those who cared to read about the issue. The new train failed to live up to the railroad's high expectations.

"We are never going out of the passenger business, but any failure to recognize the impact of competition is unrealistic."

— William White, president of NYC in an address to the New York Society of Security Analysts. Reported in *Railway Age* April 5, 1954

*T*his train will save an industry, proclaimed NYC's advertisement for General Motors' *Aerotrain* in 1955-56. The fact that the ad was run at all was an indication about the state of the American passenger train. Another concept, *Train X,* was also being promoted as the industry's savior. Both embodied the hopes of many that there was a future for the American passenger train, at a time when its future was in serious doubt.

Years later, the U. S. Government would become interested in similar projects too, through the Department of Commerce (and later the Department of Transportation), which belatedly became interested in exploring new methods of reviving the faltering rail passenger business. *Train X* was purely the creation of the private sector, however, built without the financial aid of the government.

To many in the industry, it would seem ironic that the government, which was in part responsible (through its policies) for the passenger train's demise, was actively involved in seeking ways to restore service through technological advancement. It was as though policy, technology, and economics were independent of each other and that to promote one while ignoring the others would still solve the "passenger problem." It was an indication as to how blind policy-makers could be when it came to dealing with serious problems which were in many respects their own creation.

So, why did this country need a train of the future in 1956? Hadn't the railroads only eight years before re-equipped their passenger trains? Granted, it was no secret

that the American passenger train was in trouble. Since 1948 the decline had become precipitous, but could it be reversed solely by a train of a new design? There were those who felt that a new train, however advanced in design, operated within existing regulatory and economic parameters would certainly fail, since it was believed that the regulatory atmosphere would not change.

Fewer believed that the political and regulatory environment could be altered sufficiently to allow passenger service to become profitable or even self-supporting, and that any change would be an uphill battle at best. It was apparent that if a train of the future were to succeed, it would have to do so within the existing climate, forcing its creators to seek potential solutions through the element of equipment design.

How could a train of the future become profitable, or, for that matter, was it possible at all? Passenger service, in general, had not been profitable since 1929. To answer these questions, one has to look back at railroad history for an understanding of why the railroads were in the bind they found themselves in the 1950s.

In the latter part of the 19th century, railroads had become powerful monopolies, led by industry moguls and financial speculators, men whose names are legendary—Jay Gould, J. P. Morgan, William K. Vanderbilt, James J. Hill, among others. Their reputations as being inflexible, insensitive, and ruthless when it came to business matters earned them the distinction of membership in a sinister pantheon of industrialists known collectively as "the Robber Barons."

Allied with these nefarious individuals were the investment banking houses of J. P. Morgan, Drexel, and the Mellon interests. Together they dominated and corrupted government; created and destroyed industries (and careers) as a matter of capricious personal whim — purely for their own benefit and financial gain.

Needless to say, they became very unpopular with the

J. W. Swanberg Collection

New Haven's *Comet* was an early attempt to provide a passenger service which combined a low cost of operation and a high utilization of equipment. Its double ended design feature obviated the need to turn the train at its destination. It operated into 1951. United Aircraft's Turbotrain would resurrect the *Comet's* ghost 25 years later.

Passengers were accustomed to riding trains such as the *Mercury*, seen here eastbound at Chelsea, Michigan in the early 1950s. These trains were costly to operate and were not economical to maintain.

public ("the public be damned," said William K. Vanderbilt—often quoted out of context) and this unpopularity would be perpetuated for generations—right through the 20th century.

In the mid-1800s, railroads had become inflexible authoritarian organizations, military-like in their operation and structure, reflecting the fact that the only role model for a bureaucratic structure at the time was the contemporary military. This organizational structure and management style was born out of the necessity to conduct train operations without delay or incident. Rules were developed for the safe conduct and passage of both freight and passenger trains. Their operation was predicated upon the following of orders—train orders. Failure to follow these orders could result in disaster—and often did. What evolved was the "railroad way"—"We do it this way, *because*." — End discussion.

As a result, railroad supervision kept a close eye on their employees and gave them specific instructions, often step-by-step, as to how they should perform work. The railroad was not receptive to independent thought or innovation.

Over time, railroad labor unionized to combat the caprices of the often unscrupulous managements. Since the railroads were so labor intensive and having large numbers of employees, the unions grew rapidly and eventually eclipsed the political influence of railroad management.

As the railroads grew into monopolies in transportation - which they used much to their advantage, further damag-

ing their reputations - they became such wealthy and powerful institutions that the government stepped in to curb the excesses of railroad power and financial influence. What followed was legislation establishing the Interstate Commerce Commission (ICC) in 1887 to loosely regulate the railroads. With humble origins, the ICC would, over time, expand its authority and influence.

The states, not to be left out, established public utility commissions to further regulate the railroads within their borders. One such regulation mandated that passenger trains maintain full crews, i.e. engineer, fireman, conductor, brakeman, and flagman. Such rules usually grew out of public concerns for safety and serious collisions, often which resulted from a failure in communications. More crew members ostensibly meant safer operations.

Back at the turn of the century when the railroads were this nation's largest employer, they had already established their own traditions and methods of operation. Employees were assigned specific job classifications with rates of pay which set them apart by the types of work they performed. Passenger train crews, for example, wore uniforms which depicted rank—stars, stripes and all. Everyone, from the waterboy to the president, had a title.

A crew's work day, generally determined by the operational limitations of the existing steam locomotion and union agreements, was based on 100-150 mile segments and was considered a "basic day" for passenger train crews. Engine

New Haven's *Comet* is seen at Boston's South Station (circa 1938) shortly before its run to Providence, Rhode Island, 45 minutes away - by train.

crews had separate working agreements with similar limitations. On NYC, passenger train crew change points were located on its Chicago-New York mainline at approximately 150-mile intervals.

Every time a train had to have cars cut-in or cut-out additional expenses were incurred because it required a separate switching crew (engineer, fireman, conductor, etc.) to perform the work. If a train had to be turned, it required a separate crew. All would be paid a minimum of one day's pay, according to established rules.

When the railroads were the only form of transportation in town, these payments were not considered excessive and made a railroad job a highly sought-after position.

During World War I, the government "leased" the major railroads and the U.S. Army directed their operation. It was during this period that further encroachments were made on the railroads' freedom to operate, negotiate and set rates, and pay employees, when Congress enacted legislation which established a Board of Railroad Wages and Working Conditions. This and other boards came and went as political power and influence shifted from the railroads to the unions, but perhaps the most far-reaching decision to be made by the board was the establishment of an overtime rate, to be paid after completion of an eight hour or 100-mile day, at a sum of "time and a half."[4]

The Board of Railroad Wages and Working Conditions went further to stipulate that each employee would perform certain defined tasks and that for any task beyond that, regardless in what connection, another man (the railroad was male dominated) would have to be "called" to do the work. Penalty payments would be made to both men (a day's wages for the man not called) for the railroad's failure to abide by this stipulation.[5] This gave birth to the claim, "its not my job."

Once precedent was established, it was set in stone, so to speak. Only through protracted negotiation could railroads change existing working conditions. Many times, when negotiations failed, the unions struck and the railroads shut down. Commerce came to a standstill and pressure was

The *Mercury* train of the 1930s operated into the 1950s with a matched set of equipment. The gray and silver cars presented a striking appearance. It is seen here near Chelsea, Michigan in the early 1950s.

brought upon the government to step into the fray.

Another stipulation was that railroads could not penalize or discriminate against an employee (through wages or termination) for membership or non-membership in a union. This had the effect of furthering the unions' influence.

When the war was over, the railroads not only wanted their properties back, but also greater freedom of action with a modicum of regulation to make clear the parameters within which they could operate. Naturally, the government was reluctant to dissolve the Army's agency which ran the railroads when the war was over in November, 1918. Congress wanted the Army to continue regulating the railroads and insure a smooth (and slow) transition back to private control. President Wilson, tired of the delay, and under court suit by railroad investors, announced in early January 1920 that the government's control of the railroads would end on March 1, 1920.[6]

Not entirely happy with this abrupt move by Wilson, Congress soon took action to bring a measure of order in the sale and trade of railroad securities and assuming an oversight function through the passage of the Transportation Act of 1920.[7] It gave the ICC fairly broad powers to pass judgment and restrict railroad activities, such as in construction, abandonments, operations, rates and charges, and like any governmental bureaucracy, it would choose to broaden and expand its powers in a manner consistent with whatever administration was in office (particularly through the Depression—the Roosevelt years).

Congress also established a labor adjustment board whose members were political appointees who would decide labor disputes when negotiations or arbitration attempts failed. Conflicts were thus subjected to political influence and both labor and management would become deadlocked if either side thought they could gain the advantage by having their differences settled by the board. This had the effect of further complicating work rules and compensation as well as removing the incentives to reach a separate agreement.

Title IV of the Act held important implications as far as the railroads' passenger service was concerned. It gave the commission powers to approve railroad service discontinuations which involved interstate commerce. The states followed suit and extended the scope of the public utility commissions' authority to govern in a similar fashion within state borders.

Faced with increasing competition from the airplane and automobile during the Depression, the railroads saw their passenger traffic market being challenged. The Greyhound Bus System, for example, was established in 1929. By 1930, bus lines had already cornered about one-fifth of the intercity passenger market![8] Experiencing declining revenues, the railroads sought ways to reduce costs while seeking methods of bringing back their passengers.

As early as 1934, the railroads were looking for ways to reduce operating costs and attract passengers through train design. In the Midwest, Burlington Route had introduced its Budd-built Zephyr in 1934. In the east, Boston & Maine and Maine Central introduced their Zephyr counterpart, the Flying Yankee, running between Boston and Portland, Maine. Both were streamlined and caught the public's attention, but these trains did not solely address the issue of reducing operating costs. One of the earliest experiments which would play such a significant role later on, however, was the

10

An aging NYC Hudson serves out the last few months of its service life pulling the northbound *Ohio State Limited* from Cincinnati to Cleveland on the Big Four route. This scene is north of Fairborn, Ohio (15 miles north of Dayton) in August 1955. The double track is actually single-track lines shared by the Erie Railroad and NYC.

New York, New Haven and Hartford Railroad's, "Comet." The New Haven was looking for an innovative, lightweight, high-speed, and inexpensive train to run between Boston and New York. The company which seemed as an unlikely source for a train stepped forward with a design—the Goodyear-Zeppelin Company of Akron, Ohio. The consortium was a joint-venture between Goodyear—of tire manufacturing fame—and the German Zeppelin Gesellschaft, which built the famous Zeppelin dirigible.*

The train consisted of three articulated cars which ran on four trucks. Two power cars containing 400 hp Westinghouse Model 3-E diesels with Westinghouse main generators were located on either end of the train, with a straight coach located in the middle.[9] *The Comet* was eventually restricted to a Boston-Providence route, however, because its diesel power precluded it from entering Grand Central Terminal.

The train was purchased by the New Haven for many of the same reasons which were to generate the creation of *Train X.* The New Haven was experiencing competition from the buses using the highway (U. S. Route 1 - a result of the Federal Highway Act of 1916 which established a network of publicly financed federal highways) even during the Depression, and the emerging airlines. What the railroad needed was a design which would satisfy the public's fasci-

*The association also explains why Goodyear owns a blimp.

nation with the streamline design and the railroad's need of a train with a low cost of operation.

The latter prerequisite lay in the Comet's articulated, double-ended design. The train would not require switching, nor would it have to be turned, thus eliminating those expenses associated with locomotive-drawn trains. The train experienced its problems which were common to articulated trains (if one car needed service, the whole train had to be removed from service), but was an overall success. It ran in service for sixteen years, finally being retired in 1951.

By the end of World War II, the railroads were at a crossroads. Many within the industry saw nothing but opportunity ahead and concluded that with investment in new passenger equipment the traveling public would return to the rails. There were others who were not as sanguine.

A select few saw a different future. They believed that the traditional approach to designing and operating passenger trains would have to change because the world and the public had changed. A new approach to providing passenger service would have to be devised—including forms of regulation, as well as reinventing the concept of passenger service and the manner of its conveyance. It would mean that the traditional concepts of a railroad passenger service, including equipment, as well as operating methods and pricing, would have to be completely redesigned.

One such individual was Robert R. Young.

Is White Right About Passengers?

NYC President William White and the "Passenger Problem"

RAILROAD NEWS & EDITORIAL COMMENT, May 1953

William White is saddled with one of railroad's biggest, meanest chores. He is president of the 10,700-mile New York Central, the nation's No. 2 railroad revenuewise; and the Central is sick. It's been sick since 1929 when operating revenues started a tailspin from 590 million dollars to 283 million by 1933. It took another thrashing in the recession of 1938 because one of its largest tonnage producers, the automobile industry, is extremely sensitive to the industrial barometer. And it's still sick because Central has been unable to rid its system of these inflation-swollen infections: high fixed charges, high terminal costs, high passenger deficits.

Other clouds darken William White's office hours. He has cash to push just Central's sorely needed improvements — dieselization and track overhaul — and that only by the grace of a conservative dividend policy. He must also live with the fact that somebody wants the railroad; since 1946 Robert R. Young has been bidding and biding his time for Central control, and maintaining meanwhile that the huge carrier could be a gold mine — if it had Young management.

White is awed but not avalanched by his role as attendant physician to a big

railroad which barely breaks even. He believes that Central ought to be cured, not consoled, and to that end he has seized the system by the collar and is shaking it up. He has created a passenger traffic veep, promised to restore the Century's 16-hour timecard, and appointed a liaison man between the company and its commuters. Where the road was once reluctant to part with land holdings near Grand Central, he has expressed a willingness to get out of the real estate business. Toward his stockholders he has been resolute on a ticklish issue: dividends will not be disbursed at the price of deferring track maintenance or failing to replace service-worn steam power. The press has found him a frank, factual man. And concerning Young's latest purchase of Central common, he got off a minor classic: he told a reporter he hoped it would be a good investment.

In summary, William White would appear to be man enough for a man-sized job.

In a specification, however, White would appear willing to swap long-term profits for short-term savings. He does not like the manner in which Central conducts its passenger business, which accounts for 15 cents out of each $1 of operating revenue. By the I.C.C. cost-allocation formula the road dropped 55 million dollars on its passenger trade in 1951. White, give him credit, is no slave to the Commission's yardstick. He points out that the actual out-of-pocket loss stood between 25 and 30 million dollars, which exceeded the road's total 1951 net income of 24-3/4 million. To shave, even eliminate passenger loss, White is being quoted as backing a three-way approach to the problem. He would (1) divide rather than duplicate rail service offered by two or more roads between certain cities where the trains are not now full; (2) limit ticket sales to seating capacity of equipment through an airline-type reservation system; and (3) kill off branch-line schedules which show no hope of making money.

Is White alone in his approach? He is not. Just for the record, here is what the Pennsylvania is doing: It has created a new vice-presidency "for the purpose of reducing, and ultimately eliminating, the large losses currently being suffered by the company on passenger traffic." Indeed, Eastern railroads as a group are so alarmed about their passenger deficit that a part of White's panacea is a plank in their new five-point legislative reform program. They ask the right to appeal train abandonment cases directly to the I.C.C. (state commissioners now have the final say-so on intrastate runs), and they stamp this request with the same priority they place upon such other pressing needs as a stoppage of transport subsidies and a cut in the timing lag on freight-rate hearings.

So obviously it's the scope rather than the spirit of White's thinking which makes it of headline stature today. As yet no other top-chair railroader has dared suggest a reduction in mainline passenger-train service or a retreat from the railroads' traditional role as true common carriers of passengers —— this because of the cost of maintaining stand-by equipment to meet seasonal traffic peaks. Yet this is the logical, inevitable conclusion of the industry's attitude and White is to be complimented for laying it on the line.

But is he right?

No.

The big, bad and basic fault of such reasoning is that it contrives to make the passenger suit the railroad instead of vice versa. Ever since they emerged from the wartime passenger honeymoon of a huge volume and a low operating ratio, the railroads have all but told the man in the street that they would just as soon he took his business elsewhere ——

to the automobile dealer, to the airline, anywhere but to the depot. He has been told he is a burden upon the back of the shipper and has been quoted massive I.C.C. formula deficits to prove it. He is informed that the $4 he paid for steak in the diner doesn't begin to cover the cost of preparing and serving it and he is briefed that the mail, express and baggage cars behind the engine don't meet their costs either. His average cost per mile has climbed from 1.871 cents in 1945 to 2.657 cents last year, and he can no longer buy a ticket on credit. What's more, he must pay $1 for a reserved coach seat, shell out 25 cents for a pillow, and give the red cap 15 cents per bag. Finally, he reads that the railroads can't afford to add extra cars to carry him home at Christmas or to the beaches in July, and that six round trips daily between cities the size of Chicago and Cincinnati (White's own example) could be cut back to three.

Is it any wonder that he feels neglected? Or that revenue passenger-miles skidded from 64.6 million in 1946 to 34.2 million last year and are on the downgrade again after a brief pickup due to troop movements incident to Korea? Even the competition, which has cost troubles of its own, is doubled up in laughter; Capital Airlines President J. H. Carmichael recently testified that his industry "would be glad to relieve the railroads of their troubles in this field." As opposed to climbing into the passenger tree to cut off the dead branches, the railroads have begun to saw through the trunk — and it's pretty plain to the bystanders who recall other times when they chopped off the limb they were sitting on.

Then is the passenger problem so much fiction? Of course not. No one would begrudge William White's concern over a service that contributes 15 per cent of gross, yet loses more out-of-pocket than the total company net. No one would contend that there are not those trains which defy profitable operation. No one would argue that the commutation issue lends itself to easy solution. The point is that we are devoting 80 per cent of our effort toward cutting costs and only 20 per cent toward boosting volume; and in the process we have borrowed the average man's shoulder so often as a crying towel as to verge on the biggest public-relations blunder of our time.

If we expect to stay in the passenger business (and last year it did bring almost 1-1/4 billion dollars into the railroads' cash registers, approximately 10 per cent of total receipts),

we must behave accordingly. We must place these first things first:

1. We must build volume because the railroad plant inherently tends toward higher efficiency (hence, more profit) when operated at maximum capacity. Fares, especially in the East, have been pushed beyond the point of diminishing return; it's time to at least boldly experiment in the other direction.

2. We must overcome our veteran resistance to fresh concepts of passenger equipment. The dome, for instance; it became a practical reality in 1945, yet in 1953 only one railroad is operating such cars east of Chicago. And the RDC: Major passenger haulers either insist upon buying these self-powered coaches for local runs only or stubbornly refuse to have one on the property in any kind of service. Or *Train X*: William White's admission that Central is "looking at it closely" was the first public acknowledgment by a top industry spokesman that the new-type streamliner even existed, much less might be of some conceivable benefit.

3. We must quit our back-fence bickering with the Brotherhoods, explain that we will operate more trains if full-crew contracts are repealed, and come to terms about a seniority system that presently promotes the discourteous employee and discourages the capable one.

4. We must start selling tickets on a positive plane — not on the theory that so many people need train service but that many more people could be coaxed into wanting train service.

5. Finally, we must abandon our sob-sister approach to the public — and confine our blues to where they belong; the office. In 1953 the average passenger should not have to worry himself about such purely internal ills as dining car costs — and he is not going to. He is interested in what he can get, not give, which explains why the sales technique of the airlines and the automobile makers continually catches fire.

This average passenger, this man on the street, this creator of public opinion, suspects that the railroads are not making a genuine, wholehearted, all-out effort to sustain and expand their passenger business. And he is correct.

General Motors' "Train of Tomorrow" is FRIGIDAIRE equipped

Frigidaire Refrigerators preserve food in the ultra-modern diner and provide ice cubes and cold beverages in the luxurious lounge. Frigidaire Air Conditioning keeps passengers comfortable in the "Astra Domes" and throughout the train. Refreshing drinking water from Frigidaire Water Coolers is always on tap. And each car has its own supply of electricity, provided by a "Power-Package" developed by Frigidaire in collaboration with Detroit Diesel Engine and Delco Products Divisions of General Motors.

Now see how FRIGIDAIRE can help your business!

The same skill and experience Frigidaire called upon to solve the many unusual refrigeration and air conditioning problems presented by this entirely new kind of train are available to your business. Yes, to any business or institution needing refrigeration or air conditioning equipment. With Frigidaire equipment you get the benefit of over a quarter-century of refrigeration experience, including the building of over 8 million refrigerating units . . . dependable, economical refrigeration and air conditioning equipment for hundreds of types of businesses, large and small.

So, whatever your requirements may be, consult your local Frigidaire Dealer, a specialist whose counsel is yours for the asking and whose organization is trained to engineer, install and service every installation properly. You'll find his name in your Classified Telephone Directory under "Refrigeration Equipment" or "Air Conditioning." Or write Frigidaire, Dayton 1, Ohio. Leaside 12, Ontario.

Refrigerating Units • Cooling Units • Controls • Display Cases • Reach-in Refrigerators • Water, Beverage, Milk Coolers • Ice Cream Cabinets • Air Conditioning Equipment • Household Refrigerators, Electric Ranges and other appliances.

You're twice as sure with two great names

Frigidaire *made only by* **General Motors**

3

Enter Robert R. Young

> "In 1937, I, like most men, had the idea that someday I would like to retire, and being independent, I retired. But, of that, I very quickly became tired, so looking for the easiest berth which I could find where I could make the greatest record with the least effort, I chose the railroad business."
>
> —Robert R. Young
> in a statement before the I.C.C., September 17, 1947.

The war was over and it was time to return to the pursuits of a peacetime economy. The country was retooling from the industry of war and turning its attention to supplying itself with those items denied them by the Pacific and European conflicts so recently ended. It was time to return to "business as usual." For the railroads—the nation's primary transporter of raw materials, finished products and passengers—the end of the war meant resuming normal operations and positioning themselves so as to take advantage of the anticipated surge of freight car loadings and passengers.

With the end of the World War, America's transportation picture was on the verge of undergoing a dramatic and sweeping change —for those who took the time to notice. The public, deprived of routine automobile use during the war due to gas rationing, flocked back to their cars. The automotive industry, tooled for war, converted back to resume automobile production, anticipating a booming market. Meanwhile, many in the railroad industry were seriously concerned about its own future. Hoping that their financial health would improve, they inundated the locomotive and car builders with orders for new power (diesels, primarily) and rolling stock.

Shortly after the railroads placed their orders, the nation faced severe supply shortages and recession. The labor market, once strained by the shortage of adequate supply, was experiencing a glut due to the return of its soldiers, and tension arose between management and labor as unions

Robert A. Hadley
The southbound *Cleveland Mercury* is seen at Trenton, Michigan in 1950 with one of the former *Century* engines of the 1938 edition. The effect of streamlining in the Art Deco style gave the appearance of a railroad which had its eyes on the future.

Engine 4917 blasts the *Mercury* near Delray, Junction in 1939. Engines of this period were accorded cast NYC oval plates in the pre-adhesive days. To many this was "futuristic" railroading.

pressed for increased wages and benefits. This impacted the railroads, too.

Unfortunately for them, the world was a different place than it was before the war and instead of a business as usual, the railroads would find themselves scrambling to cut losses. What they seemed unable to do was reshape their way of conducting business.

New York Central, the Pennsylvania Railroad and other eastern carriers had to vie with one another to divide a diminishing flow of freight and passenger traffic. In the case of passenger traffic, the railroads followed the traditional approach to attract business: outfit the luxury trains with new equipment on faster schedules.

They quickly learned that there was no longer as much traffic as they had assumed. The anthracite coal mines of Pennsylvania were depleted; much of the east's industry was moving west and south; and increasing amounts of high-rated

freight traffic were being shipped in trucks. While air travel was still in its adolescence, it was gaining popularity. The automobile, once a local transport option, was also gaining adherents as a long-distance carrier which offered greater independence and substantially lower costs. At the same time, the automobile manufacturers were conducting glamorous advertising campaigns which extolled the virtues of the automobile.

The world had changed, and for the most part, the railroads had not. A few in the railroad industry were vocal about the need for reform and restructuring, but reform nevertheless. Some recognized the need but didn't know what to do about it. Others felt that the industry was out-of-date and what the railroads had to do was "return to the drawing boards." Among the latter was R. R. Young.

Robert R. Young, a clever, savvy, and resourceful financier, had earned a reputation of reinvigorating financially troubled railroads which he controlled through his purchase of the former Van Sweringen railroad empire's Alleghany Corporation, which controlled the Chesapeake & Ohio Railway, the Erie, the Missouri Pacific, the New York, Chicago & St. Louis (Nickel Plate),* the Pere Marquette, and the Wheeling and Lake Erie Railroads. Young and his partner, Woolworth fortune heir Allan Kirby, were majority stockholders of Alleghany and, therefore, controlled its destiny.

Young represented a new breed of industrialist, a corporate raider. "I would not call myself an executive or a railroad man, but I would call myself a security analyst..."[10] With his roots in the investment community, Young and his Alleghany Corporation were viewed as a threat to the existing establishment. Where once the railroads had been a singularly dominant force in both industry and the economy, backed by the investment banks, Young typified the shift in the corporate culture which made the railroads increasingly subservient to outside control and pawns in a high stakes chess match with other corporations, such as Young's Alleghany.

After the war, in 1945, Young wanted to expand Alleghany's holdings to include the Pullman Company, which operated the vast majority of sleeping cars across the nation, when it was placed for sale following the anti-trust decision of 1943. By controlling Pullman, Young believed he could use the company as a forum to launch his crusade to alter the industry and improve its ability to become profitable.

The Pullman case was of historic proportions and it held significant implications for the future of the industry and New York Central.

Since 1924, Pullman, Incorporated owned both the Pullman-Standard Car Manufacturing Company and its operating division, the Pullman Company. The basis of the federal suit, filed under the Clayton and Sherman anti-trust acts, was that the Pullman Company's refusal to service the sleeping cars of any other manufacturer (i.e. The Budd Company) constituted a monopolistic practice. This monopoly, the suit charged, stifled competition and removed the incentive to improve passenger cars and services.[11] The suit was filed on July 12, 1940 and it would take another seven years to sort out. Just the same, the ownership of Pullman by Young was vital to his plans.[12]

The suit claimed, in part:

A substantial part of all sleeping car travel involves the use of connecting carriers. Even if a railroad could prepare to operate its own sleeping car service, it would be unable to send its sleeping cars over the lines of connecting carriers with which the Pullman Company has contracts, or if these Pullman contracts were abrogated, without then entering into numerous complicated contracts for exchange of cars.

* Nickel Plate reputedly drew its name from the initials of its name, N.Y.C., (St.)L. and the popular plating process.

The Pullman Company has plenary power to deprive railroads of sleeping car service and to force undesirable rolling stock and onerous terms on recalcitrant railroads. No railroad of any size can afford to be deprived of Pullman service or to be discriminated against ... This power of the Pullman Company is so great that its very existence, apart from any threats or positive action by the Pullman Company ... is alone sufficient to force railroads ... to comply with policies favored by the Pullman Company.

Defendants have stifled competition in the manufacture, sale, lease, and operation of modern lightweight, streamlined, high-speed trains and rolling stock ... and defendants have unreasonably retarded the growth and development of a supply of modern passenger coach and sleeping cars in the United States.[13]

Although the initial decision was rendered on April 20, 1943, it took the court another year before it instructed Pullman, Incorporated to sell one of its divisions. Pullman chose to divest itself of the Pullman Company by selling it, but it had to decide to whom it would sell. With court scheduling delaying the proceedings, it wasn't until March 1945 that the court gave Pullman another year to dispose of the assets. So, between 1943 and 1946, Young would maneuver to purchase the company, taking up the suit's complaint as his standard. By mid-1945, with the war in Europe having just ended and V-J Day within sight, the battle for Pullman was heating up.[14]

One of the arguments which Young effectively employed in 1945 was that the rail passenger in this country was still restricted in movement because of the policies by the cabal of railroads, the Pullman Company, and the finance moguls which controlled them. Indeed, upon close examination one found that among the members of the Pullman Company's board of directors were representatives of the New York Central, the Pennsylvania Railroad, the Erie, the banking houses of J. P. Morgan & Company, Chase National Bank, Bankers Trust Company, New York Trust, Guaranty Trust Company, National City Bank, and First National Bank of New York. Young pointed to these interconnected interests as proof-positive of his arguments regarding the investment community's control of the railroad industry - an element of control which he felt had to be broken.

With ownership of Pullman under a Young regime, he contended, passenger service would rebound in popularity and use. He promised to invest heavily in new passenger equipment which would be the zenith of luxury travel.

The battle for Pullman, meanwhile, was contentious. When it became clear that Young was a viable contender for the company and might actually win control of it, the task of organizing the opposition fell to Willard F. Place, vice president of finance of New York Central. Place, a Pullman board member, formed a buying group (an alliance of railroads) in

Trains such as NYC's fabled *20th Century Limited* were re-equipped with modern passenger cars soon after World War II. That alone was not enough to bring passengers back to the rails. Yet, people have longed for the trains they so quickly abandoned in favor of the airplane and automobile. When they remember the trains of the "old days," this is what comes to their minds.

September 1945 to counter Young's bid. Young was not pleased with this move.

Facing the growing opposition of the railroad and investment banking communities, which feared the power of Young's influence were he to gain control of Pullman, he took his campaign for the Pullman Company to the national press. In a series of populist advertising campaigns, beginning in November 1945, he gained national prominence and earned a name for himself as a crusader for the small investor and the traveling rail passenger. He would later employ similar tactics in his fight for New York Central.

One of his first assaults concerned the railroad industry's transcontinental passenger traffic. True coast-to-coast rail travel, he claimed, was impossible because a passenger had to change trains (and cars) in the process, namely at Chicago, St. Louis, and New Orleans. Young argued that those traveling by air were not hampered by such restrictions, which only enhanced the popularity of the airlines to the detriment of the railroads.

His advertisements berated the railroads for not allowing passengers to travel cross-country without changing trains. It wasn't a bad idea, really, and actually made sense. He challenged the eastern carriers by announcing that the C&O and the Nickel Plate would institute such a service. Only, there wasn't a lot of traffic that wanted to travel

cross-country by rail, what with the rising popularity of air travel. And realistically, the C&O and Nickel Plate simply didn't have the passenger market to undertake such a venture.

The most famous of the press campaigns came in the form of an advertisement which featured a hog, cigar in hoof, riding past the rail traveler under the heading, "A hog can cross the country without changing trains, BUT YOU CAN'T!" The ad first appeared on March 4, 1946 and struck a responsive chord among the public.

New York Central, the Pennsylvania, and the Baltimore and Ohio, felt the competitive pressure and scrambled to come up with cooperative agreements with the western carriers to provide "coast-to-coast" service. On the C&O, however, it wasn't long before it became apparent that there just wasn't much demand for it, and in June 1948 the C&O abandoned the through-car service (to St. Louis) it had initiated in 1946.

Young was unharmed by the experience. He had made his point, but since there was little traffic in C&O's cross-country market, nobody took notice when it was discontinued.* Not surprisingly, Young was earning a reputation of a maverick, but the industry learned not to ignore him.

Unfortunately for Young, despite all his maneuvers in the

* While not a coast-to-coast service, as Young was promoting, few noticed that it was only a "through-car" service. Young had a skill for such deceptions - and got away with it.

The *Train X* prototype coach unit was placed on display at several locations on the C&O. This view offers a good look at the car's profile. The circular windows contrasted with the conventional rectangular window design of the modern coach and was another feature borrowed from the *Talgo* coaches.

press and the courts, Pullman accepted the buying group's offer and on December 18, 1945 the federal court approved the sale. Undeterred, Young would vainly continue his battle in the press and by appealing the decision to the ICC and the Supreme Court* while blaming the Wall Street interests for his failure.[15]

Even before the lower court's decision was rendered, however, sensing that he would fail to win control of the Pullman Company, Young turned his attention to another forum where he could promote his beliefs and innovations for the rail passenger trade. If the Pullman Company would be denied to him, then he would reach for what he considered to be another bastion of influence and power—New York Central.

Through C&O, Alleghany began to buy NYC stock. Young and Kirby also acquired stock personally, and began a quiet bid for representation on NYC's board of directors. Fearing that Young might be successful in his bid, but not wishing to engage him in a corporate death-match, the anti-Young forces at NYC came up with a plan. In a strategic cor-

porate maneuver, NYC's President Gustav Metzman shrewdly offered two positions on his board to Young and C&O's president, Robert Bowman, wagering that the ICC would block the application on the grounds that this would create an interlocking directorship—an illegal business practice.[16]

Again, Young was denied his quest, this time by the ICC. Its decision motivated Young to plan his next moves for a takeover of the property. While simultaneously plotting to take stock control of NYC, which he knew someday would be his, Young continued to pose as the savior of rail passenger service. He was still in control of the C&O, however, and would use that railroad as his platform - for the time being.

Young pursued his dream of making C&O a showpiece when it came to its passenger operation, despite the fact that its passenger trains did not have the markets or handle the volume of a New York Central or Pennsylvania. He wanted to create the passenger service which was, "second to none." The C&O confidently undertook to replace its entire passenger car fleet with orders from Pullman-Standard and Budd. It quickly regretted the move, however, when a coal strike curtailed profits and made paying for the new equipment very difficult. The C&O had to cancel much of its

* The ICC approved the sale on February 1, 1947; the Supreme Court rendered its decision in favor of the buying group on March 31, 1947.

undelivered order, and after a couple of years found itself having to sell off many of the cars which had been delivered, even those built for the all-Budd stainless-steel *Chessie*, a train ahead of its time.

The silvery stainless steel liner included innovative features and was the epitome of luxury daytime travel by train. Young even had a trio of steam-turbine-electric locomotives specially constructed to pull the Chessie across the Alleghanies between Washington, D. C. and Cincinnati. Unfortunately for Young, the economy and the existing traffic base weren't conducive for such a bold venture.

The *Chessie*, Young's dream, was quietly stored after delivery and a promotional tour. Sadly, it never ran a mile in revenue service.

The C&O was not alone. All across America, the traveling public was turning away from the passenger train and Young was quick to make an assessment that the railroads should be doing more to lure the public back to the rails.

When C&O canceled its highly-publicized revamping of its passenger fleet in 1948, Young had to find a scapegoat and blamed the passenger car builders for numerous delays and the inflated cost of the cars. Then he added a new dimension to his argument when he told his board of directors that the existing technology was out-of-date, and what the railroad(s) really needed was an innovative new train of advanced design to compete with the rising popularity of other modes of travel.

Young felt that what the railroads needed were fresh ideas to combat traditional approaches and methods; if the industry was to survive, it must change with the times.

As far as Young was concerned, the railroad industry was not moving ahead as effectively and fast as he thought it should. Upset by his failure to win control of the Pullman Company and the lack of support he received in the process from the Association of American Railroads (AAR), Young withdrew C&O from the organization in 1946. Young and his railroad were isolated, at least diplomatically.

This did not deter Young, who set out to create a separate association which would more aggressively pursue the

ideals and agenda which he had in mind. Young established the Federation for Railway Progress (FRP) in early 1947 with the avowed purpose of encouraging "free competitive enterprise in the interest of the traveling and shipping public, the railroads, their employees, and the nation's defense."[17]

The new Federation would, in the public interest, take action:

1. to inform the public about all matters pertaining to American railroads, and particularly to keep before them the facts regarding any deterrents to the full accomplishment of the purposes of the Federation;
2. to modernize railroad equipment and facilities and otherwise improve railroad passenger and freight services so that the public will have available a more efficient transportation system in the interest of the national safety and the public convenience;
3. to bring about an equitable balance among wages, return on investment, and rates in the railroad industry so that employees, investors, and the shipping and traveling public will all receive fair treatment;
4. to staff railroad management with progressive, energetic, efficient personnel who have full confidence in the future of railroads in the United States;
5. to abolish monopolistic practices and bring about the return of free enterprise to the railroad industry.

As the Federation's president, Young appointed Thomas Deegan, Jr., vice president of passenger and public relations of C&O. Thomas Deegan began his career as a correspondent with the New York Times. He later became an employee with American Airlines and where he caught the attention of Robert Young who asked him to become a railroad executive with Chesapeake & Ohio Railway. Deegan was a trusted and influential advisor to Young and helped him recruit the talent he needed to run his organization.

Young also established an advisory committee which was made up of nationally known figures to assist in the programming of the policies of the Federation, which included former secretary of state, Edward R. Stettinius, Jr., Claire

---

A Hog Can Cross America Without Changing Trains—But YOU Can't!

The Chesapeake & Ohio and the Nickel Plate Road again propose to give humans a break!

It's hard to believe, but it's true.

If you want to ship a hog from coast to coast, he can make the entire trip without changing cars. You can't. It is impossible for you to pass through Chicago, St. Louis, or New Orleans without breaking your trip!

There is an invisible barrier down the middle of the United States which you cannot cross without inconvenience, lost time, and trouble.

560,000 Victims in 1945!

If you want to board a sleeper on one coast and ride through to the other, you must make double Pullman reservations, pack and transfer your baggage, often change stations, and wait around for connections.

It's the same sad story if you make a relatively short trip. You can't cross that mysterious line! To go from Fort Wayne to Milwaukee or from Cleveland to Des Moines, you must also stop and change trains.

Last year alone, more than 560,000 people were forced to make annoying, time-wasting stopovers at the phantom Chinese wall which splits America in half!

End the Secrecy!

Why should travel be less convenient for people than it is for pigs? Why should Americans be denied the benefits of through train service? No one has yet been able to explain it.

Canada has this service . . . with a choice of two routes. Canada isn't split down the middle. Why should we be? No reasonable answer has yet been given. Passengers still have to stop off at Chicago, St. Louis, and New Orleans—although they can ride right through other important rail centers.

It's time to pry the lid off this mystery. It's time for action to end this inconvenience to the public . . . NOW!

Many railroads could cooperate to provide this needed through service. To date, the Chesapeake & Ohio and the Nickel Plate ALONE have made a public offer to do so.

How about it!

Once more we would like to go on record with this specific proposal:

The Chesapeake & Ohio, whose western passenger terminus is Cincinnati, stands ready now to join with any combination of other railroads to set up connecting transcontinental and intermediate service through Chicago and St. Louis, on practical schedules and routes.

The Nickel Plate Road, which runs to Chicago and St. Louis, also stands ready now to join with any combination of roads to set up the same kind of connecting service through these two cities.

Through railroad service can't be blocked forever. The public wants it. It's bound to come. Again, we invite the support of the public, of railroad people and railroad investors—for this vitally needed improvement in rail transportation!

Chesapeake & Ohio Railway · Nickel Plate Road
Terminal Tower, Cleveland 1, Ohio

The *Train X* experimental coach was connected to a special transition car (a rebuilt C&O caboose), which was coupled to one of C&O's regular intercity coaches (delivered by P-S only four years before) and powered by a C&O—ex-Pere Marquette—E-7, No. 106. The demonstration runs earned the *Train X* project the credibility it desperately needed at this stage.

Booth Luce, Admiral William F. Halsey, M. Lincoln Schuster (of Simon & Schuster Publishing), and a former governor of New Jersey, Charles Edison.

Young said that he would like to see everyone, "from farmer to industrial worker, represented in the Federation." He also stated that he hoped that the advisory committee would "keep us on the straight and narrow path, and never take a selfish interest."[18]

Young noted there were serious problems which the AAR was not aggressively addressing. His contention was that the problems facing the railroad industry (not just passenger trains) were not exclusively competition from other modes of transportation. Two of the chief factors working against the railroads were the low rates of return allowed by the ICC and the control being exercised by those whom Young called the "dambankers."

Since 1929, the ICC enforced a 3% ceiling on the rates of return on railroad investments, compared with 6% for public utilities and even higher rates of return for unregulated industries and the airlines. In 1955 American Airlines, for example, was earning a 7.9% return; Eastern Airlines, 7.6%; United Airlines, 6.9%; while Greyhound Bus was earning 5.4%. Even the Class I highway truck industry was earning more - 4.5%![19] Young argued that this discouraged initiative and hindered capital investment for innovative improvements.

He also contended that the ICC was ponderously slow in approving rate hikes, train abandonments, and most other matters brought before it. The manner in which the commission conducted business would itself have to be streamlined.

As far as the banking interests were concerned, Young argued that his nemesis, the investment banks, were exercising too much control over the railroads in contrast to their other interests, such as the airlines. This power and control severely handicapped the railroads from more earnings.

Young's campaign was intended to correct this state of affairs by garnering public support to pressure the ICC to allow the railroads greater freedom in setting rates, conditions of service, and the ability to make a profit. In addition, he reasoned that this would also reduce the influence of the investment bankers by giving more freedom to railroad executives to control the business and the industry's destiny.

Naturally, the banking interests were unsympathetic and succeeded in imposing their will on the ICC.

Meanwhile, the passenger train had to compete with a newcomer - the airplane - which offered the advantage of time. Much of the physical plant required for the airlines' operation was provided through low-cost government capital with consequential costs subsidized by the local, state and federal governments. This allowed the airlines to offer a superior service at a lower cost than the railroads could offer. For example, the cost of a 1957 airline ticket between Chicago and New York was less than a first class Pullman ticket. Since the airplane had the train beat over the long distance, Young believed that the train should focus on the short to medium distance market and offer competitive savings in travel time and cost as compared with the automobile. Therefore, the train would have to increase its speed and reduce total trip times.

Existing equipment had its limitations, he said. Young disparaged the rail passenger cars then under construction as being "top heavy." In point of fact he noted, GM's 1947 domed

"Train of Tomorrow," then on a promotional tour around the country, demonstrated his contention. More importantly, he felt that the cost of the railroad passenger car was too high relative to its earning capacity.

So, a new train would have to be invented - a totally new concept - a high-speed *Train X* which would cost less to build, operate and maintain; have more rapid acceleration, deceleration, and have a lower center of gravity in order to accommodate curves; reduce total trip times; and be able to run over existing rails without the need to invest in extensive track improvements. In order to be high-speed, the train would have to be of light weight—considerably lighter than existing equipment.

Young had seen a design for such a train which had operated in Spain during the war, the Spanish *Talgo*, and he became its chief proponent. "Progress" became his crusade, and *Train X* would be his vehicle to changing the industry.

Young claimed that the *Train X* design would take the best of the *Talgo*'s design and make improvements. *Train X* would weigh about one quarter as much as the average train and cost about half as much to build and one third as much to operate. A comparison of costs per seat between the average automobile and the rail passenger coach highlighted Young's argument.

The 1950-era automobile weighed about one and one-half tons and carried five or six passengers comfortably. The weight per seat came out to about one-third of that for the railroad passenger car. The same automobile cost about $2,600 (in 1950 dollars) or $650 per seat.

The typical 60-seat coach in 1950 weighed approximately sixty tons, or about one ton per seat. When the locomotive weight, about three hundred tons, was added to that of the cars in the train the average weight per seat rose to roughly one and one-half tons.

C&O Historical Society

An unidentified mechanical department employee examines the *Train X* test car's wheel and suspension.

The average passenger coach cost about $135,000, or approximately $2,300 per seat. Add in the locomotive's portion and the cost rises, above $2,600. Of course, diners and sleepers raise the cost even more.

Young argued that the railroad had to lower its investment and operating cost per seat in order to remain competitive. In effect, trains had to become lighter, faster, consume less fuel and be less costly to operate and maintain.

Meanwhile, Deegan was also concerned about the continuing decline in the variety and quality of passenger services being offered to the traveling public. He used his considerable influence with Young to impress his boss with a credible and crucial argument: that passenger service was increasingly becoming subservient to the convenience of the railroad and not to the passenger. He postulated that if the passenger train were to attract business, it had to become (what we would call today) "user friendly." Deegan's ideas became Young's battle cry.

Deegan recognized that there was a change occurring in the interest and needs of the market for railroad passenger service. When the railroad was the primary source of intercity transport, the industry offered four types of train service: commuter; short haul (within 200 miles); medium haul (200-500 miles), and long haul (over 500 miles). Traffic profiles covered the whole spectrum of passenger travel needs, each with established trip requirements for the railroads to meet.

The trains which the railroads offered to travelers contained amenities and special services aimed at those who were expected to use them. For example, NYC's *Mercury* trains were daylight, medium haul trains which catered to business and casual travelers, families, etc. Many overnight trains were being patronized only by those to whom the element of time was most important, namely those on business—who did not want to travel during business hours.

NYC's *20th Century Limited* was a posh overnight train which catered to the businessman. Deegan argued that luxury trains such as the *20th Century Limited* must ultimately cater to the interests and needs of the casual traveler, not unlike the Burlington's *California Zephyr*.

Deegan was one of the few who realized that the profile of the average traveler was in transition and he convinced Young that the airplane and automobile were draining away the mainstream of the railroad's passenger traffic primarily because they offered the patron more of what he wanted and needed at an affordable price. If passenger trains were to maintain their profitability, they would have to serve the public's needs. Those needs had to be identified and, if necessary, addressed by a wholly redesigned service. NYC's passenger studies of 1956-58 would confront this issue and their recommendations would eventually influence the course of rail passenger service developments in this country 20-30 years later.

In 1948, the trains were still catering to their traditional but shrinking markets. The railroads' response was to promote the new services. By the early 1950s, the losses were so great that the railroads cut services

These railroad officials are out for a ride. The interior of the test car looked rather Spartan in comparison with conventional equipment.

arguing that it was the fault of the passenger. While this was partially true, it wasn't a popular position to take and bordered on arrogance.

The railroads have never enjoyed a good reputation with the public, in a general sense, although this was more of a problem with the eastern railroads than in the west and south. While they tried to stay in its good graces when the passenger trains were popular, they have suffered under the reputation of its aforementioned barons of industry. Blaming the railroad's troubles on its patrons only added to its troubles.

To fulfill his dream of a new train, Young turned to Kenneth Browne, a design engineer from Wright Aeronautical Corporation, whom he had installed as research director of C&O in December 1944. The aviation industry was where the design talent was drifting, so if a new train had to be designed it would have to come

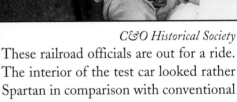

This view allows us to see the air and electrical connections associated with the coupling arrangement, as well as the lowered dolly wheels which allowed the car to be moved when disconnected from the train.

The test car undergoes closer scrutiny as the car's chief designer, Kenneth Browne (5th from left) looks on.

from outside the railroad establishment. It should be no surprise that the experimental cars had an airline "look" to them.

A native of Boston, Browne pioneered the design of an aircraft oil cooler and directed the initial flight testing of high altitude supercharging technology. He was awarded the Wright Brothers Medal in 1939 and contributed to the development of gasoline fuel injection systems, among other accomplishments.

He graduated from the University of Colorado in 1926 with a Bachelor of Science degree and served for two years as an instructor in electrical engineering laboratory courses at Cornell University in their College of Arts and Sciences.

Browne brought in a staff, including a young and visionary engineer from the University of Cincinnati, Alan Cripe.

Young gave them orders to design a lightweight train meeting all current construction and safety standards which could operate safely at high speeds on existing track, that would be inexpensive to build, operate and maintain, and *would attract passengers.*

Cripe went to work on the initial design while the C&O approached both Pullman-Standard (P-S) and American Car & Foundry (ACF) to test their interest in developing the lightweight train concept. ACF was already building the *Talgo* for the Spanish National Railways and, therefore, was interested. Designs for C&O would eventually include sleeping and dining cars as well as coaches, but were never built (although the *Talgo* cars built for Rock Island would include a dining car).

P-S was also interested - dark clouds were on the car builder's horizon - and offered to build a prototype car at its own expense.* It seems that the only thing better than wholesale is free, so C&O joined in a collaborative effort with P-S.

It was at this point, while *Train X* was in the development stage, that Young announced the cancellation of about a third of C&O's passenger car order declaring, "deliveries have been so incredibly slow that we have had to cancel orders to keep up with our own research."[20]

C&O and P-S built a mock-up of the proposed train (under the auspices of the FRP) and even went so far as to take publicity photos to generate interest. The cars were exhibited at the Chicago Railroad Fair in 1948 and 1949. Soon thereafter, P-S began construction of the prototype coach for a test run.

Young had pushed the patience of the industry with his criticisms of its lack of vision. He solicited membership in his Federation for Railway Progress and through its publications and advertisements heralded the arrival of his new train. But because he had stepped on so many toes, he had difficulty in gaining adherents to his ideas. Help was around the corner, however.

The prototype car was tested on February 21, 1951 when it made its initial run between Pullman's Hammond plant to Griffith, Indiana. The car was attached to a transition car - rebuilt from a retired C&O caboose (No. 90599) - which was coupled to one of C&O's venerable self-propelled coach-combine "doodlebugs." A second test run was made on May 25, 1951 between Griffith and LaCrosse, Indiana at which time Young and officials from P-S rode the car.

After further refinements, on May 8, 1952, it made a test run between Grand Rapids and Grand Ledge, Michigan.

*By the end of 1948, approximately 1,840 passenger cars were on order - some placed as early as 1944 - but not yet delivered. By mid-1948 the railroads had ordered 184 additional passenger cars, but in the last three months, only 14 additional cars were ordered. Young projected that the end of the passenger car industry was within sight, a forecast not lost on Pullman-Standard.

Another demonstration run was made for the benefit of executives from fourteen other railroads on June 11, 1952 between Detroit and Plymouth, Michigan - a distance of 48 miles - behind one of C&O's standard EMD E7 passenger locomotives, for the sake of appearance and speed. During these test runs, the test train reached a top speed of 105 mph. Pullman-Standard's corporate magazine claimed, "In fact, open bottles of pop, which were placed at various locations in the car, demonstrated the excellent riding qualities of the coach. They did not overbalance, shift, or spill any of the contents during the high speed periods."[21]

On October 16, 1952 C&O's president, W. J. Tuohy, made a presentation to the Eastern Railroads' Presidents Conference. At that meeting, NYC's new president, William White (who took office on August 1, 1952 - Metzman was elevated to chairman of the board), agreed to approach the presidents of the Pennsylvania Railroad, the Baltimore & Ohio Railroad, and the New Haven Railroad, about joining in the *Train X* project.

Following the meeting in October, another test run of the car was made on December 18, 1952 between Detroit and Plymouth. With the prototype car in the test mode and commitments from General Motors to provide a locomotive, the interest which Young had been trying so hard to generate was finally beginning to take shape.

Then the project stalled. For in the meantime, while keeping up the battle for an improvement in C&O's passenger service, Young had become consumed with a new, yet familiar, battle—control of New York Central.

C&O Historical Society
The *Train X* coupling would include the train's electrical connections as well as the air line for braking. The design was carried over to the *Xplorer* and *Aerotrain* to obviate the need to have mechanical forces make the couplings manually.

On May 25, 1952 the car made a demonstration run behind a C&O "doodlebug," a standard self-powered coach/baggage/RPO combination car - the first run was to demonstrate the car and not how fast it could travel. *Below:* At Griffith, Indiana passengers stepped off for a look. Robert Young is at left with Pullman-Standard's D.R. Carse.

Pullman-Standard Assistant Vice President D. R. Carse (left), Robert Young (middle) and Kenneth Browne (right) confer during the May 1952 test run of the Train X test car. Young's flamboyant nature extended to his taste in neckties, apparently.

"Optimism"

"At long last there is even some room for optimism—albeit long-term—about the passenger side of our operations, which has cost your company and the industry so dearly for more than a decade. The concept of a low center of gravity, lightweight passenger train, so long in the mind and heart of our chairman, Robert R. Young, and popularized by him as the 'Train X' concept, has been on our list of preferred projects since the new management took over the Central.

"Although we are very hopeful of the results this new passenger equipment will bring about, it is not enough to solve our problem. The evils built into the hodge-podge of unequal taxation, regulation and subsidization of the various competing forms of transportation not only result in lavish handouts of tax money and facilities to our competitors, but frustrate us in our efforts to provide the type of service the public wants at a price the public is willing to pay. In cooperation with the rest of the railroad industry, we are seeking a return to fair competition in the transportation industry."

—*Alfred A. Perlman, NYC president, in the road's
1955 annual report to stockholders.*

C&O employees and others examine the mock-up coaches which were being exhibited at the Chicago Railroad Fair of 1949.

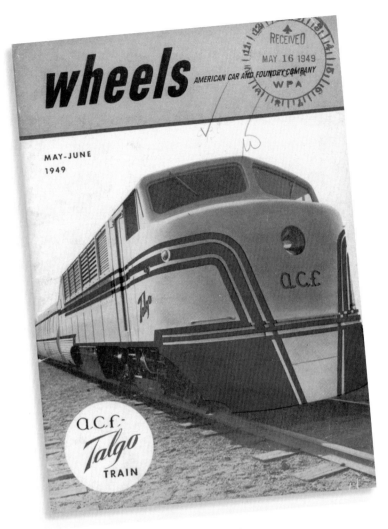

RENFE Train No. 3 is seen crossing the Manzanares River as it departs Madrid, Spain on November 5, 1959.

4

Talgo

"We would breath much easier if we felt certain nobody would buy them."

— a Greyhound spokesman commenting on *Talgo*, quoted in *Railway Age*, January 4, 1954.

American Car & Foundry (ACF) had entered lightweight train production in 1946 with a patented articulated design called *Talgo*. *Talgo* was actually the result of a privately funded project inspired by a Spanish army engineer, Alejandro Giocoechea, who approached a wealthy Spanish philanthropist, Lucas de Oriol, with his idea to commission the design of a new lightweight train for use on the Spanish National Railways. The train drew its name from the Spanish Tren (train), Articulado (joined), Ligero (light), Giocoechea (its inventor), and Oriol (the name of the Spanish philanthropist). He claimed that the design would be revolutionary and would restore a profit to its operators.

Giocoechea had identified several factors of train operation which he wanted to improve upon. Not only did he wish to lower construction, maintenance, and operating costs, but he also wanted to increase the train's speed. These issues he would address through the elements of train design.

A major issue which had to be addressed was the centrifugal forces which combine to offset the train's equilibrium. On curved track these forces tend to accentuate the train's top-heavy design causing it to want to roll over. For this traditional aspect the railroad engineers compensated with super-elevation, or tilting one side of the curve with a slight speed restriction causing the train to tilt at the same angle as the track. The benefits of these tactics, however, are offset by the comfort requirements.

One of the underlying problems of trains is that their speed is limited by their ability (or inability) to move through curves without reducing speed. On average, the cost to re-align curves for high speed passenger trains to save a few minute's time is disproportionate to the benefits gained. But in the U.S., a curve which is tilted for high speed passenger trains poses a hazard for slower speed, top-heavy freight trains, making them more vulnerable to tipping over. Giocoechea wanted to design a train which could handle existing curves without major reconstruction of roadbed alignment. *Talgo's* design was intended to reduce weight and

Collection of J. W. Swanberg

On June 27, 1954 ACF's *Talgo* demonstrator was at New Haven, touted as "tomorrow's train." Its cars were shorter than those to be built by P-S for the *Xplorer* and *Daniel Webster*. There doesn't appear to be much interest in the new train. *The Senator* is making its station stop in the background.

J. W. Swanberg

New Haven's *The New Yorker* is westbound at Woodlawn in the Bronx on July 17, 1957. The Fairbanks-Morse EDER-7 "Speed Merchant" locomotive leads 12 ACF *Talgo* coaches. A twin locomotive is on the train's opposite end in the "push" mode.

to have a significantly lower center of gravity so both of these primary factors would keep the train on the rails at higher speeds. Since lighter equipment could tend to be unstable, Giocoechea designed a method of linking (coupling) the cars together so they would act as a single unit, yet still be free to bend when rounding curves.

During World War II, a 5-car test train was constructed and tested on the Spanish National Railway system. The results were significant enough to persuade the Oriol family to back the project. Not having the industrial capacity to build another such train, the Spaniards looked to the United States for assistance in its construction.

At the end of 1944, Giocoechea contacted a mechanical engineer, James J. P. MacVeigh who secured the interest of ACF (on behalf of Oriol's new company, "Patentes Talgo S A") to construct two train sets. The specifications called for a low-slung articulated and lightweight (aluminum) train powered by a single locomotive containing an 1150 hp Hercules diesel engine. Two 110 volt A.C. auxiliary engines generated power (50-cycle, 3-phase A.C. power) for lights, heat, and air conditioning.

ACF, which also built the *Talgo* locomotives, relied on the lower center of gravity to allow the locomotive to take curves at higher speeds as well, since its center of gravity was two feet lower than that of a stan-

Courtesy Simmons-Boardman Publications A comparison of the cross sections of the Association of American Railroads standard and the *Talgo* design shows the difference in car height and center of gravity.

10'-2"

10'-0"

13'-6"

10'-10¼"

A.A.R. CENTER OF GRAVITY

A.A.R. FLOOR

TALGO CENTER OF GRAVITY

5'-4"

TALGO FLOOR

4'-3"

3'-6"

2'-2¹/₃₂"

RAIL LINE

dard passenger engine. This reduction lowered construction costs, but just as important, weight and wind resistance, which combined to produce greater fuel economy.

Design work on the train began in January 1946, with actual construction taking place at ACF's plants in Berwick, Pennsylvania, and in Wilmington, Delaware. The all-coach, 370 foot-long train carried 176 passengers, but did not carry any "speciality" cars such as a diner or lounge. Rather, meal service was provided "airline" style, with each passenger so desiring a meal being served at his or her seat.

Each coach "unit" was 20 feet 2 inches long, coupler to coupler, and 10 feet 4-3/8 inches wide and carried 16 passengers. The observation unit was 7 feet 2-1/2 inches longer. A rubber gasket, or diaphragm, encircled the ends of the cars using a specially designed zipper making the interior appear to be like one long tube, without partitions. This unique feature of the train eliminated the use of vestibules between the cars.

A single set of wheels was located beneath the couplings between cars, and rotated on their own bearings—not on an axle. Brakes were similar in design to an automobile's, expanding against the inside of the wheel's hub. Retractable five-inch dolly wheels were located at one end of each car to be used when the cars were detached or switched out or in.

Two *Talgo* train sets were exported to Spain and went into service on July 14, 1950 with Spain's fascist dictator, Generalissimo Francisco Franco presiding over the festivities. A third set, consisting of six cars and locomotive (the whole train was only 168 feet long), was built for ACF's own de-monstration purposes. The train went on tour and generated interest, but there weren't any buyers.

In time, however, similar newly designed *Talgo* cars were sold to the Rock Island for

ACF, Author's collection

ACF - *Talgo* locomotives were constructed at Berwick, Pa., and had an adjusted height of 12 feet, resulting in a 14% lessened wind resistance. Three locomotives were built.

use with its Aerotrain/Rocket locomotive; and to the New Haven (for its *John Quincy Adams*) and to the Boston & Maine. The latter two would be powered by locomotives built by Fairbanks-Morse, which it called, "Speed Merchants."

In 1996, a new and improved , built in Spain, commenced a six month demonstration service between Seattle, Washington and Portland, Oregon. The demonstration proved so successful that three additional train sets have been ordered for use in the Pacific Northwest corridor services between Seattle, Portland, Eugene, and Vancouver, supported by the Washington and Oregon State Departments of Transportation and operated by Amtrak. Their popularity has many people thinking that the trains will bring the public to the rails and off the highways.

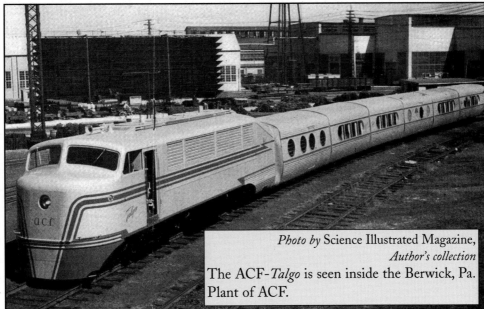

Photo by Science Illustrated Magazine, *Author's collection*
The ACF-*Talgo* is seen inside the Berwick, Pa. Plant of ACF.

All: *Photo by* Science Illustrated Magazine, *Author's Collection*

Units of the *Talgo* were coupled together at the center and supported by two load-bearing members on the forward unit. Additional couplings consisted of power, brake and water lines, inner and outer diaphragm zippers of a self-sealing type, as well as steel safety cables.

Below: The cars had rubber self-sealing diaphragms. One is being examined by ACF's director of research and development, J. M. Gruitch (left) and *Talgo's* U.S. representative, James MacVeigh.

Five-inch dolly wheels folded back under the car when the car was coupled to the train, and were lowered when the unit would stand alone for servicing.

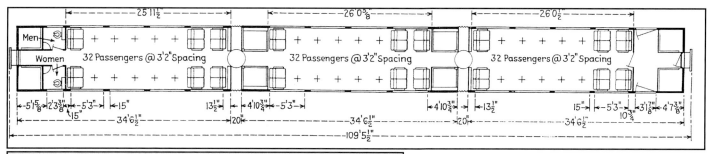

Courtesy Simmons-Boardman Publications
Above: The floor plan for the 3-unit *Talgo* coach

All: *Photos by* Science Illustrated Magazine,
Author's Collection

Left: The uncoupled *Talgo* unit shows the floor design. Passengers had to negotiate the narrow passage between the supports and the wheels.

Right: One of the concerns which the new trains addressed was the ability to allow passengers to board and alight from the cars without the need for stepboxes. The lower floor level made access easier.

ACF, Author's collection

Left: This photo was taken to demonstrate the low level of the new coaches on the *Talgo,* but it also offers the reader a nice view of the interior of the train. While ahead of its time, the *Talgo* train did not gain any adherents in the U.S., and Spain was its only customer. A newer and improved design of the coaches did not enhance sales beyond the Rock Island, New Haven and Boston and Maine Railroads.

Aerotrain was striking in appearance and it was hoped that it "would save an industry." While it was mechanically sound, its poor ride proved to be its major shortcoming.

By late 1952, General Motors began developing its version of a lightweight train, which it called *Aerotrain*. Always interested in expanding its markets, GM felt that if a new type of passenger train were to be developed, it should be a GM product, pulled by a GM locomotive.

Among the many corporations which supplied the railroad industry and which, perhaps, exerted the most profound influence on its destiny, General Motors would be at (or at least near) the top of the list. So, when it came time to develop *Train X,* it was not a surprise to learn that GM was involved in some manner. After all, GM had been in the forefront of the "new trains" enterprise as recently as 1947 with its "Train of Tomorrow."

While much time and expense had been spent on the design and creation of a prototype car beginning in 1946, it wasn't until the early 1950s that a sense of urgency motivated railroad executives to pursue the concept of a lightweight, high performance train in earnest, fueled by increasing passenger deficits and declining ridership. When the test runs of the prototype car were made the time came to look at motive power.

GM became interested in supplying a locomotive for *Train X* in late 1952 when EMD notified the officials at C&O that they would develop and provide a locomotive at its own expense. In a report from a luncheon meeting at the Greenbrier Hotel, dated October 20, 1952, J. S. Marshall of the C&O's legal department wrote:

General Motors has definitely decided to take over the design and building at its expense of the locomotive for *Train X.* This will be an engineering development project of considerable magnitude. It requires an analysis of the size, weight and speed of the train and the servicing requirements for heat, water and electric power. The locomotive will be built on the cross-section of the *Train X* car rather than the present diesel locomotive cross-section. The EMD representatives are enthusiastic about joining in this partnership. The time is ripe for such a venture when passenger deficits under the ICC formula are on a constant increase. ICC commissioners, coal operators and other freight shippers are continually throwing barbs at the railroads about these heavy passenger losses, subsidized by the freight business. Only

Bob Lorenz

In July 1956, the *Aerotrain* was switched from its Chicago-Detroit schedule to a Chicago-Cleveland run. The *Aerotrain* made a scheduled stop at Sandusky, Ohio where there were plenty of curious onlookers, but fewer passengers.

Aerotrain's locomotive contours were a blend of the then current GM styling from its automotive division. This photo, taken at Sandusky, Ohio, contrasts the new train and the slogan on the boxcar at right.

through a research program as *Train X* can the railroads answer the criticism that freight traffic is paying for the passenger losses and the railroads are doing nothing about it.

The cars for *Train X* will be built at railroad expense. The C&O board has already apportioned funds for a demonstration train and several other railroads have indicated an interest in joining in the project and sharing the cost.

Mr. Tuohy [president of C&O] stated that he had proposed to Mr. Osborne [vice president, General Motors] that General Motors carry through the whole project, both locomotive and cars, in order to maintain continuity and drive, the cost of the cars being borne by the railroads. Mr. Osborne said he would consider this, there being several problems about building the cars, such as plant capacity.

Arrangements were made to have Gene Kettering, EMD's chief engineer, meet with Mr. Browne [C&O's design engineer for *Train X*] in Cleveland, Wednesday, October 22, to go over tentative designs for the locomotive.

The Rock Island ultimately became the first customer of GM's newly designed locomotive when in 1954 it announced that it had ordered a *Talgo*-type "Jet Rocket"

The "News Briefs" from the New York Central HEADLIGHT July-August 1956

...The Central's lightweight train that has been running in experimental service between Chicago and Detroit was switched to a Chicago-Cleveland run July 15. The change was made as part of a plan to test the new train under varying traffic and market conditions.

On its new schedule, *Aerotrain* leaves Cleveland daily at 7:35 A.M., Cleveland Daylight Time, and reaches Chicago at 1:15 P.M., Chicago Daylight Time. Returning, it leaves Chicago at 5:00 P.M., reaching Cleveland at 11:45 P.M.

On the westbound run, *Aerotrain* makes regular stops at Linndale, Elyria, Sandusky, Port Clinton, Toledo, Bryan (all in Ohio), Waterloo, Kendallville, Elkhart, Mishawaka, South Bend, LaPorte and Gary (all in Indiana).

On the eastbound run, the train stops at Englewood, Gary, LaPorte, South Bend, Elkhart, Waterloo, Toledo and Linndale.

Aerotrain's new schedule is effective to and including September 29. On its eastbound run it represents a "new train" service, while westbound it replaces the *Lake Shore Limited*, which now terminates at Cleveland.

which would operate between Chicago and Peoria. The locomotive would be of the *Aerotrain* design, but the (four 3-articulated unit) cars would be built by ACF, based on an improved Talgo design.

The new Rock Island train, which entered service on February 11, 1956 cost approximately $600,000. What GM produced was a locomotive with a distinctive appearance, which also contained separate diesel generators to power lights, heating and air-conditioning.

The locomotive was powered by a standard V-12 1200 hp 567C diesel, mounted within an all-aluminum carbody with a two-motor, four-wheel truck leading and a single two-wheel idler axle trailing truck. It had a fuel capacity of 800 gallons. Two Detroit diesels, Model 6-71 engines with Delco alternators, provided 120kw of 440 volt, 60 cycle trainline power for lighting, air conditioning and heating. While it was never built, a "B" unit locomotive was considered which would have had the outward appearance of one of the coach cars.[22]

Having the capacity to build the car bodies, GM decided to offer a train set of its own design utilizing many of the standard components then in use by its bus division. GM approximated the cost for its all-GM component train to be about $100,000 less than the

"Changing Times"

Excerpted from "Is the Passenger Train Obsolete?" by David P. Morgan
Copyright 1956, Kalmbach Publishing Co.,
reprinted with permission from the July, 1956 issue of TRAINS magazine.

"The paradox of the railroad passenger business is that revenues are sliding at the very moment that ...

... The nation's population, employment, payroll, and travel urge are at an all-time peak.

... Rail travel is — or should be — at a peak of safety, comfort, speed and convenience.

... There is an impressive list of selling tools in the railroad camp: credit cards, rent-a-car plans, automation and mechanization of ticket sales and accounting, improved research and advertising aids, 88.4 per cent dieselization, and a variety of new equipment.

"There's nothing wrong with this passenger, business," sums up Monon's Warren Brown, "but our thinking, specifically this gloomy pessimism that oozes into every sentence and comment about passenger business."

For instance:

The problem will not be solved by exclusively blaming declining sales on circumstances beyond the industry's direct control, e.g., subsidized competition, Federal excise taxes, the high cost per seat of new coaches. The prospective rider doesn't care and traffic will have vanished by the time all such ills have been cured — even assuming all of them can be cured.

There's a danger in expecting too much of the new experimental lightweights because, to date, the design emphasis has been loaded in favor of meeting the railroads' demands and not the passengers'. In return for their reduced costs certain of these trains threaten to subtract from the space, riding qualities, and feature extras of existing equipment. To quote an engineer, it may be a case of one road saying to another, "It costs us less to operate our empty train than it does your empty train."

Between them, the paved highway and the plane have radically altered the customer's concept of travel. Item: the railroad mind still tends to think of Chicago and St. Louis and New Orleans as "gateway" cities—where railroads terminate and everyone changes trains. Not so the customer, what with nonstop flights and belt highways that completely bypass metropolitan areas."

Paul Stringham, M. D. McCarter Collection

Rock Island's *Jet Rocket* is racing through Sankoty, Illinois on July 24, 1957 on its run between Chicago and Joliet. The *Talgo* cars are from ACF and include coaches, lounge and a dining car.

H. H. Harwood, Jr.

The *Aerotrain* pauses at East Cleveland to pick up members of the local press in early January 1956 when the train was on tour.

Rock Island's train, or $500,000. Each car was to cost about $32,000.[23]

The design for the independent cars was GM's standard 40-passenger aluminum bus body, slightly widened (by 18 inches) riding on a steel underframe on two single-axle trucks. The cars were modified to use the bus driver's space for an entrance and the bus engine area for a lavatory and a food service pantry. Like the bus, luggage was carried in 150 cubic-foot compartments located under the floor section, accessible from outside the car.[24]

Each 40-seat coach unit stood 10-feet, 9-inches high and was 9-feet 6-inches wide and weighed 27 tons. Suspension

New Trains

Excerpted from "Is the Passenger Train Obsolete?" by David P. Morgan
Copyright 1956, Kalmbach Publishing Co., reprinted with permission from the July, 1956 issue of TRAINS magazine.

THE PROBLEM: Many railroads — particularly those in the East — do not think any money can be made in the passenger business with existing equipment because of high initial cost, high maintenance, and high operating cost per seat. Example: Pennsy's Jim Symes doesn't think one of the $250,000 sleepers operated in coast-to-coast service is capable of making money even when fully loaded.

THE PRESCRIPTION: Following a group study attack on the problem by six roads, carbuilders have come up with six basic designs: tubular, hi-level, improved RDC, Talgo, *Train X* and *Aerotrain*. Four of these ideas incorporate lower centers of gravity, drastic reductions in gross weights, head-end auxiliary power, closer seating, new suspensions, etc. All will be in revenue service sometime this year. As compared with previous equipment innovations, the major difference is that more stress is being laid on cost reduction than solid passenger comforts. Because of limited power on most of the trains and existing signal and right-of-way restrictions, little can be expected in improved schedules. Nevertheless, the new trains incorporate wholesale new thinking and, if New York Central's spokesmen are right, will put the profit back into the passenger picture.

NYC's *Aerotrain* is seen on Cleveland's east side just before a test run for the local press in January 1956. A few days later it made its official debut in the Windy City.

on the *Aerotrain* was similar to that of a GM bus, air-filled bellows inflated by the train's air line. (A similar but improved suspension would later become standard on Amtrak coaches.) In the event of an air leak or when the air bled out of the bellows due to standing, a rubber pad was provided for supporting the car load after a 1-inch deflection.[25]

The main heating systems of the cars were electrical. An auxiliary heater was supplied on each car - an oil-fired hot water heater fed by a 40 gallon fuel tank located on each car to be used as supplemental heat during extreme cold. Fuel

consumption for the train, i.e. lights, heat, propulsion, etc., was estimated to be approximately one gallon per hour for normal operation. The independent oil-fired units on each car were estimated to burn about the same amount of fuel.[26]

Repair costs were estimated to be $.66 per unit mile. This was based on a cost of $2000 per unit per month and an average mileage of approximately 22,700 miles per unit per month, multiplied by .75, which was the ratio of the number of cylinders per unit in the lightweight train to the number of cylinders in the average Santa Fe locomotive.[27]

It was assumed by GM that the average train speed would be 60 mph, and at that rate the fuel consumption would be approximately 49% of that for a standard locomotive.

The locomotive and train, interestingly enough, was not designed to operate in reverse - it was not double-ended. This deficiency was to be rectified in any future production, but in the meantime it would not address the cost savings issue of turning the train - a significant drawback.[28]

Two train sets were built for demonstration purposes—Nos. 1000 and 1001. Locomotive 1000 (and its train set) was delivered to the Pennsylvania Railroad which operated between New York City and Pittsburgh, Pennsylvania, while locomotive 1001 and its cars went to NYC for service between Chicago and Detroit, and later Chicago and Cleveland.

Each train was designed to carry ten cars, but ran with fewer—one coach from each set was sent back to GM for testing while another was held aside as a spare. Each train set featured a futuristic observation car which looked like a cross between the trunk of a 1956 Cadillac and something out of the early 1950s science fiction classic, "The Day the Earth Stood Still." They sported white and red tail lights and the letters "GM" between them when delivered, although the Pennsylvania removed the letters on its train set observation so as to not conflict with its keystone herald which figured prominently on the rear just below the windows and above the lights.

One of the trains' featured concepts was that maintenance would be reduced by having obsolescence "engineered in." GM's carbody was easily replaceable and could be removed from its undercarriage and replaced with a new carbody about every seven years. Such a design concept, Young proclaimed, would make the economy recession-proof!

Initial test run results were mixed. The train's riding qualities indicated that "laterals" were "very bad " when operated at 100 mph.[29]

The train's creation did fulfill most of the same criteria as Young's *Train X*. It would be lightweight (made of aluminum), and have a low center of gravity; but it was not articulated like *Train X* and Talgo, and while it could run on existing railbeds, high-speed travel was doubtful.

How well it performed in service on the existing railbeds would be demonstrated, much to the disappointment of GM, Young and the public.

Proposed Schedule For General Motors' Aerotrains

As of October 1955 (subject to change)

Aerotrain 1001

Santa Fe
March 1 to March 8 - railfan trip,
Chicago to Los Angeles; on-line exhibits

Union Pacific
March 8 to March 22 - exhibits at Las Vegas (9th);
Salt Lake City (10th); Ogden (11th); Portland (12th &13th); Seattle(14th);
Tacoma (15th); Boise and Pocatello (16th); Cheyenne (17th);
Denver (18th); Topeka (19th); Kansas City (20th);
test run Omaha to Cheyenne (22nd).

Southern Pacific
March 23 to April 4 - California exhibits.

Illinois Central
April 8 to April 12 - on line exhibits.

Chicago & North Western
April 13 to April 18 - on line exhibits.

Great Northern
April 19 to April 25 - on line exhibits.

New York Central
April 27 to July 30 - revenue service, Chicago-Detroit.

Aerotrain 1000

Pennsylvania
February 26 to May 29 - revenue service, Pittsburgh-New York.

Canadian National
June 2 - exhibit in Montreal.

Southern Railway
June 7 to June 11 - on line exhibits (receives train at Washington).

Seaboard
June 12 to June 16 - on line exhibits (receives train at Atlanta).

Baltimore & Ohio
June 21 to June 24 - on line exhibits (receives train at Washington).

Wabash
June 26 to June 30 - on line exhibits (receives train at Chicago).

Missouri-Kansas-Texas
July 1 to August 3 - revenue service from Kansas City to Dallas:
option for additional revenue service August 4 to September 2 from
San Antonio to Dallas (receives train at Kansas City).

"The Cost of Doing Business"

Excerpted from "Is the Passenger Train Obsolete?"
by David P. Morgan
Copyright 1956, Kalmbach Publishing Co.,
reprinted with permission
from the July, 1956 issue of TRAINS magazine.

"It costs more than $400,000 to buy a diesel to haul the load that a $50,000 Pacific did back in 1925; and the cost per seat in the coach behind has climbed from about $300 to $2,000 or more. Wages are up, terminal taxes are up, fuel and other supplies are up — but the average revenue per passenger-mile is down from 2.96¢ in 1924 to 2.6¢ last year. Moreover, the railroad remains the one public passenger transport totally unaided by Government relief through either direct or indirect subsidy."

The Aerotrain

"The Central's fast, lightweight *Aerotrain* introduces dozens of delightful new ideas to railcoach travel. The *Aerotrain's* coaches are lower and shorter (half the length of a normal railroad car) — yet wonderfully roomy and sumptuously comfortable. And there'll be food service available for everyone!

Daily operation for the *Aerotrain* between Chicago and Detroit begins April 29th, for a trial period — a preview that lets you sample America's newest train!

Though not primarily designed for speed, the *Aerotrain* can top 100 mph with ease and comfort, while you enjoy a smooth, level ride on its bellows-like air suspension system — at no extra fare!"

NYC Form 1001, dated April 29, 1956

Collection of Bob's Photos

The Pennsylvania Railroad received a similar *Aerotrain* set. It also ran in experimental service and experienced the same problems with its ride. The Pennsy's passenger deficit was often larger than that of its biggest rival and the railroad was seeking similar solutions to the "passenger problem."

GM's Aerotrain, A New Concept

Electro-Motive Division's design is new from pilot to tail lights - Objectives: 400 passengers, 600,000 pound; conventional cost reduced by half; styling to dramatize the new departures.

The broad objectives for the General Motors *Aerotrain* were determined by conversations between various railroad presidents and N. C. Dezendorf, vice president of General Motors and general manager of Electro-Motive Division. They asked Mr. Dezendorf for suggestions that would reduce equipment investment and reduce operating and maintenance costs; lower the center of gravity and increase average speed; improve riding comfort; and make possible lower fares to attract greater passenger traffic.

Three overall objectives were set up as guides for the design:

1. The locomotive and ten cars should be held as near as possible to 600,000 lb. gross weight.
2. Both investment and operating costs of the new train should be reduced. The objective was to design coaches which could be built for approximately half the cost of conventional railroad equipment.
3. The styling should dramatize the train as an entirely new concept in passenger train equipment and heighten public interest in it.

Here, for the first time, was an opportunity to design an integrated train to match it with the most economical prime mover to obtain the ultimate in utilization and economy. An auxiliary power source in the locomotive supplies current not only for train lighting, but for individual heating and air

H. H. Harwood, Jr.

The *Aerotrain* has departed East Cleveland and is proceeding to Union Terminal in downtown Cleveland.

The *Aerotrain* is making a regular stop at North Philadelphia on its run from New York City to Pittsburgh in June 1957. The westbound train left Penn Station at 7:55 a.m. with a 3:25 p.m. arrival in Pittsburgh. It would turn and depart at 4:05 p.m. for an 11:30 p.m. arrival back in New York.

conditioning units in each car as well. Elimination of steam lines makes possible the use of an automatic coupler on the cars which makes all necessary electrical and air connections as the cars are coupled.

Freedom from problems of interchange permitted the design of an entirely new air brake system with substantial reductions in cost and weight as fundamental objectives.

Since total weight of the complete train was limited to approximately 600,000 lb, design of the *Aerotrain* locomotive was started by determining the minimum horsepower needed to pull this weight at a maximum speed of 102 mph.

The 12-567C engine, delivering 1,200 hp for traction, was found to be adequate to meet the performance requirements. This meant that the single locomotive unit needed to haul the 10-coach, 400-passenger train would be, in effect, half of a model E9 (the standard General Motors 2,400-hp diesel passenger locomotive unit powered by two 12-cylinder, 567C engines).

It was also determined that two Electro-Motive D-37 traction motors could carry the load, and this in turn led to design of the rear locomotive truck as a single idler axle which contributed to overall weight reduction.

The locomotive employs proved components of construction to the greatest extent feasible. The underframe consists of two fishbelly I-beam center sills which serve as main carrying members for the carbody, cab and equipment.

Two side sills, supported by the center sills, partially support the cab and carbody framing and skirt arrangements. Coupler pockets are welded to built-up platform constructions between the center sills. The complete underframe assembly is of all-welded construction. Outside finish consists of a light-gage sheet steel welded over a structural framework.

Main propulsion equipment is the 12-567C diesel engine, standard Electro-Motive D-15E d-c generator, and two D-37 traction motors on the front axle truck. The propulsion engine and the main generator are placed in the depressed fishbelly section of the underframe to lower the center of gravity.

In the nose of the locomotive two auxiliary power units are mounted, supplying electric power for train lighting, heating and air conditioning. They are six-cylinder Model 6-71 Detroit Diesel engines powering 440-volt, 3-phase, 60-cycle, Delco AC generators.

Several improvements in control devices have been incorporated in the *Aerotrain* locomotive. The transition-control relay is modified to keep the power higher during very rapid acceleration, and to load the power plant more effectively, on areas of moderate- to high-speed operations at reduced throttle. Motor cutout control has been improved so that, with one traction motor cut out, practically full power capacity of the other motor can be uti-

Photographer Bob Lorenz caught the *Aerotrain* at Huron, Ohio along NYC's main line on what appears to be a windy summer's day after the train was switched to a temporary Cleveland-Chicago run in 1956.

lized over a relatively wide speed range, while, at the same time, current will be limited to a reasonable value for starting and accelerating.

Car Design Factors

In designing the cars, Electro-Motive engineers started with a strong steel underframe that would carry strength right out to the sides. Underfloor compartments provide space for heavy baggage and housing for the individual heating and air conditioning units and other equipment.

The standard GMC 40-passenger intercity-type highway-to-coach body was adapted to the *Aerotrain* car with minor modification, mainly in increased width and in adding railroad vestibules at each end. This body, susceptible to fast production with all standard type components, satisfies the weight problem and also meets safety requirements.

To achieve improved riding comfort, the patented General Motors Truck & Coach Division "air-ride" was selected and adapted to railroad use.

In consideration of the objective of reducing maintenance costs, the cars were designed as simply as possible with smooth exteriors and smooth interiors, reducing the cleaning problem to a minimum.

Each car is 40 feet long, 9 feet 6 inches wide, and 10 feet 9 inches high. The floor is 43 inches above the rail—nearly as high as conventional railroad coaches. The center of gravity, however, is only 45 inches above the rail, close to that of other lightweight trains. Wheelbase of the four-wheel under-

carriage is 25 feet 3 inches. Weight of an empty car with complete supplies is approximately 30,000 lb.

The doors and steps of the vestibule at the front of each coach are arranged so the entrances will serve either high or low station platforms. At the rear of the car a lavatory is installed on the right side. Across the aisle, space is provided for a galley or snack bar for serving light meals or refreshments. In the experimental trains, four cars are equipped with different types of service to try the reception of each.

Electropneumatic sliding doors controlled by a sensitive door edge are set in the vestibule bulkhead at the front end and in the rear end bulkhead. Inner and outer diaphragms are applied to each end of the car.

The passenger compartment of the GM car has 40 seats of the modern reclining type. They are rubber filled with changeable nylon covers, washable headrests, footrests and ashtrays in the arm rests. Seat spacing is 35 inches. Package racks on each side of the car above the seats provide approximately 140 cubic feet of storage space.

Interior lighting is by a single row of fluorescent lights running the length of the car over the center of the aisle. Aisle lights are also provided on the seats. Reading lights for each seat are located under the package racks.

The interior finish is attractive and durable, requiring a minimum of painting and maintenance.

The car for the new *Aerotrain* comprises a replaceable body, which is very low in first cost compared to conventional cars. Undercarriage is expected to last many years with a minimum of maintenance. General Motors expects that when the car requires overhaul (about every seven years in the case of conventional cars), the old body can be replaced with a new one, including all the modern advances then required, for less money per passenger than is now spent for repairing and refurbishing conventional type cars.

Air-Ride System

Eight air bellows, mounted four on each single-axle truck, support the entire weight of the car. The bellows are attached to air boxes, built into the underframe of the car, which are charged with air from the train supply line.

The air-ride system consists basically of two separate charging lines, a signal device, air reservoir and ride control devices along with the necessary limit valves and check valves. The arrangement is shown schematically in a diagram.

Initial charging of the air bellows is through a line which bypasses the 75-psi limit valve, air reservoir and ride control valves. A limit valve in the line limits its charging pressure to 30 psi. The line assures an initial charge in the air bellows before the air brake system at 60 psi is charged. It also acts as a lower limit for the air-bellows pressure for normal operation. A relay air valve connected between this line and the signal line operates a signal in the locomotive whenever the bellows pressure is below 25 psi.

The main charging of the air bellows and ride control devices is done through the air-reservoir line. A 75-psi limit valve in the line keeps this system from drawing air until the brake system is fully charged. The air reservoir supplies air to the system when pressure in the train supply line is reduced, as in a full brake application. A second limit valve, after the air reservoir, limits the maximum charge in the air bellows to 35 psi.

The air pressure in the bellows is controlled between the upper and lower limits by the ride-control valves, which act to hold the height of the carbody above the rail at a con-stant value. When the load on the car is increased, the valves admit more air to the bellows; and when the load is decreased, the valves exhaust air from the bellows. Three valves are used, two at the front corners of the car and one at the center rear. This gives, in effect, a three point suspension control which holds the car parallel with the rails, both longitudinally and laterally. A hydraulic dashpot is incorporated in the ride control valves to delay the pneumatic response. This allows normal springing to take place without constant readjustment of the bellows air pressures.

The *Aerotrain* has a unique air conditioning and heating system, designed by Electro-Motive engineers, which eliminates the need for a steam generator in the locomotive and the trainlined steam supply required with conventional equipment. In each lightweight car a self-contained air conditioning system is installed. The system includes a 5-ton Frigidaire refrigeration unit with a reheat cycle for dehumidification and temperature control.

Located in the equipment compartment in front of the rear wheel well on the car undercarriage, the system is controlled from a panel in the snack-bar compartment of the car and may be manually set for either heating or cooling cycles or for straight ventilation.

Conditioned air is distributed through longitudinal ducts along each side of the carbody at the floor line and thence to vertical ducts which disperse the air through openings at the base of the windows. Outlets are provided in the longitudinal ducts for distribution of air over the floor. Air is returned to the conditioning unit through ducts in the floor. Twenty per cent make-up air is obtained through grills in the roof and is transmitted to the air conditioner through vertical ducts in the rear bulkhead of the passenger compartment. The system has a total air flow capacity of 2,070 cfm.

Heating is supplied as required by a water-to-air heat-transfer coil. During the heating cycle, heat is supplied

---

"Passenger Train Costs"

From NYC 1957 Annual Report

It is in passenger operations that the steep, continuing rise in costs, especially labor costs, has its most serious impact. Opportunities for more efficient utilization of the workforce are limited by "full crew" regulations and other circumstances beyond management control. As the Central's experience during recent years has shown modern equipment, improved service, and aggressive advertising can increase traffic volume and revenue — but in a period of inflationary labor and material costs, all too often more traffic simply brings larger passenger deficits. These conditions make prompt, realistic adjustment of passenger fares to reflect current costs essential if excessive losses on this class of service are not to threaten the solvency of the entire system.

During the past year the ICC granted permission to increase certain fares. First class fares were raised five per cent in January 1957 and an additional 20% toward our original request for a 45% rise in sleeping and parlor car transportation fares. In January 1958 coach fares were increased another five per cent, to offset partly the higher wage rates that took effect the previous November.

We are also bringing our rates for other passenger operations, including such services as baggage, locker and red cap fees, up to levels more nearly approximating costs.

A year-long study of mail handling and transportation costs completed in April 1956 showed that the Eastern Railroads needed, at that time, an increase of 26% in mail rates merely to cover costs, and a 59% increase for a reasonable return on their investment. Although the case was filed with the ICC in July, 1956, a final decision is still to come down.

---

to the water by an 8-kw electric immersion heater of 28,300 BTU per hour capacity. When more heat is required, the entire load is taken over by an oil-fired heater of 150,000 BTU per hour capacity. Car temperature is controlled by a thermostatically controlled bypass valve which varies the flow of hot water through the heat-transfer coils.

During the cooling cycle, the refrigeration unit runs continuously at full capacity. Temperature control is obtained by reheating the refrigerated air with the same hot water system used in the heating cycle. In this case, however, heat for the water is obtained from the hot freon leaving the compressor by means of a pre-condenser. The amount of reheating is controlled by bypassing the water flow as necessary, and the same temperature control thermostat is used for both heating and cooling cycles.

Air-Brake System

The fact that the locomotive and cars are to be operated as a unit and coupled with automatic couplers permitted simplification of the air-brake system, resulting in significant cost and weight savings.

To further reduce weight and cost, non-metallic or plastic brake shoes were chosen for the *Aerotrain*. These shoes require only one-third the force of cast-iron shoes to produce a given braking action due to higher friction values obtainable. This made possible the use of much smaller brake cylinders than would otherwise have been required.

The arrangement is essentially a straight-air brake with variations that permit the operation of two to twelve cars in multiple service. Break-in-two protection is provided in event of the train's parting. Arrangements also have been made so that a standard locomotive could haul the *Aerotrain* in an emergency and maintain adequate air-brake control.

There are two principal circuits in the system which are

trainlined through all cars: the straight-air line and the supply line. There is also a conventional signal line. Air is supplied to the cars at 110 psi through the supply line to the application relay and break-in-two protection relay. The straight-air line controls the application relay on each car. This relay regulates the maximum air pressure supplied to the release and application brake cylinders and the volume reservoir. This pressure is predetermined, depending upon the retarding rate desired, and is nominally 60 pounds.

The release and application cylinders are of the same area and mounted so as to oppose each other in operating the brake linkage. The force of the release cylinder is applied through a slightly longer lever arm than that of the application cylinder, so that when the pressures in each are equal, the brakes are released.

Operation of the control handle in the locomotive allows air pressure to develop in the straight-air line. This reduces the regulated air pressure which the relay valve supplies to the release cylinders at the rate of 3 psi reduction for every 1 psi increase in the straight air pressure. Pressure in the application cylinders and volume reservoir remains the same because of a check valve in the line. Thus, the brakes are applied with a force proportional to the pressure differential between the release and application cylinders which is dependent upon the reduction made.

The time required for application or release has been kept to a minimum on the *Aerotrain* by the arrangement of equipment and small volumes of the brake cylinders. A full application is in effect 3.75 seconds after movement of the brake-valve handle. A service application of 45 psi is in effect within five seconds on the tenth car.

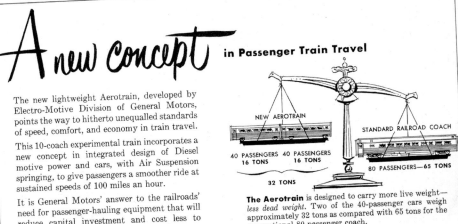

A new concept in Passenger Train Travel

The new lightweight Aerotrain, developed by Electro-Motive Division of General Motors, points the way to hitherto unequalled standards of speed, comfort, and economy in train travel.

This 10-coach experimental train incorporates a new concept in integrated design of Diesel motive power and cars, with Air Suspension springing, to give passengers a smoother ride at sustained speeds of 100 miles an hour.

It is General Motors' answer to the railroads' need for passenger-hauling equipment that will reduce capital investment and cost less to operate and maintain.

NEW AEROTRAIN — 40 PASSENGERS 16 TONS / 40 PASSENGERS 16 TONS / 32 TONS

STANDARD RAILROAD COACH — 80 PASSENGERS—65 TONS

The Aerotrain is designed to carry more live weight—*less dead weight*. Two of the 40-passenger cars weigh approximately 32 tons as compared with 65 tons for the conventional 80-passenger coach.

Aerotrain—Center of gravity is 10 inches lower than in present standard railroad coaches — yet passengers ride no lower than in conventional trains and considerably higher than in other projected lightweight trains to provide a more enjoyable view of the scenery.

4.3% of Intercity Travel Was by Rail

Copyright 1955 Simmons-Boardman Publishing, reprinted with permission from Railway Age, November 26, 1955

Railroads got only 4.3% of 1955's intercity passenger business as measured by passenger-miles. More than 88% of the year's intercity travel was by private automobile.

These, and like figures for other agencies of transportation, are set out in the accompanying table, reproduced from "Transport Economics," published by the ICC's Bureau of Transport Economics and Statistics.

As the table shows, the business of railroads and bus lines was down from 1954. Air carriers increased their business by 16.2%, but their proportion of the total rose less than one-half per cent. Water carriers about held their own according to the report.

Volume of intercity passenger traffic in passenger-miles by kinds of transportation, 1954-1955

Transport Agency	Passenger Miles (billions) (billions)		Percent Change 1955 from 1954	Per Cent of Annual Total	
	1954	1955[1]	1954[2]	1954	1955
Railways, steam, diesel, and electric	29.5	28.7	- 2.6	4.7	4.3
Motor vehicles:					
Motor carriers of passenger	25.6	25.1	- 1.9	4.1	3.8
Private automobiles	548.8	585.8	+ 6.8	87.8	88.2
Total	574.4	610.9	+ 6.4	91.9	92.0
Inland waterways, including Great Lakes	1.7	1.7	+ 2.2	0.3	0.3
Airways (domestic revenue service and pleasure and business flying)	19.6	22.7	+16.2	3.1	3.4
Grand Total	**625.1**	**664.1**	**+ 6.2**	**100.0**	**100.0**

[1] Preliminary estimates
[2] Percentages computed before rounding

Testing the Cars

Testing of various components of the *Aerotrain* was carried on as development progressed. When the first car underframe was built, it was provided with a shell upper structure and was stress tested. The structure was loaded vertically up to 200 per cent of normal with no indications of abnormal high stress. The car was also loaded with 600,000 lb. buff load, applied longitudinally on the end of the car, without showing signs of distress.

After the stress tests, the car was provided with trucks, windows and doors and equipped with instrumentation for road testing. For this purpose, pickups, connected to an oscillograph, were provided for measuring the vertical deflections between the trucks and carbody. A gyroscopic instrument was installed for recording the roll of the car. Three-way ride recorders were utilized to record lateral and vertical shocks and, in addition, a television set with a camera focused on the contact point between wheel and rail was used to show how the car was tracking.

To insure that the road test gave a true picture of the performance of the car, it was coupled in between two underframes riding on the same kind of trucks and ballasted to the same weight as the test car. Tests of this train were run on railroads at speeds up to 100 miles per hour. The first test runs were by no means perfect. Subsequently, however, improvements were made, largely in the air suspension system and the accompanying shock absorbers, which greatly improved riding qualities. Experimental work in this line is being continued.

Because of the novelty of the four-wheel suspension in high-speed service, the original test train was provided with means of guiding the axles around corners. Road testing proved, however, that this arrangement was not necessary; so in the interests of simplicity it was eliminated.

General Motors emphasized that the *Aerotrain* is an experimental train and development work has not yet been completed. Achievement of the results indicated in this paper must be proved by exhaustive tests. Two identical *Aerotrains* are scheduled to begin demonstrations and tests on the Pennsylvania and New York Central. Thereafter one train will be made available to eastern railroads, beginning with the New Haven, and the other to western railroads, commencing with the Santa Fe.

It is believed that a year or more will be required to complete these tests. At the end of that time, performance, economies, and customer appeal characteristics should be well-established.

NYCSHS Collection, courtesy of H. Lans Vail, Jr.

Xplorer's diesel hydraulic engine was slightly smaller than the standard freight and passenger locomotives of the period, as can be seen in this view taken at Collinwood Shop on April 15, 1956. Unfortunately, No. 20 would become a frequent visitor to the Collinwood Shop forces who coined derisive nicknames for it, such as "Xploder," and "Mickey Mouse."

J. Parker Lamb

GM's *Aerotrain* was sent across NYC's system after its debut in January 1956. On a frigid winter's day the train was photographed in the Dayton, Ohio station.

NYC's Trains of the Future

> *"It is on the basis of Mr. Young's record, therefore, that we question his ability to arrive at sound policies and we believe he is not qualified to direct the operation of New York Central... Your present management is not interested in power... You have a choice between a promoter type of management and an experienced professional railroad management."*
> — William White, president of NYC in a letter to stockholders, printed in *What manner of man is Robert R. Young?*

> *"Let us be very sure we consider these trains but the first of a great fleet which will not only preserve the present volume of railroad passenger travel, but vastly increase it."*
> — Robert R. Young, chairman of NYC, as quoted in *Railway Age*, May 7, 1956.

New York Central had a passenger operation which far exceeded that of C&O, which even Young admitted was better suited for carrying coal than passengers. NYC and its passenger service would occupy Young's attention, and for eight years he made certain that his second fight for the company would not go unnoticed by the public and that this time he would succeed.

White and the NYC board continually rebuffed Young, who retaliated by making a nuisance of himself whenever the railroad's profits slipped or when he saw an opportunity to accuse its officials of shoddy management. All the while, he kept buying NYC stock and professing that the company could be run better and make more money if he were in control.

By October 1953, the country had slipped into another recession and by year's end NYC's revenues were lower than the year before; its passenger deficit rose to $52 million dollars. Young saw his opportunity and planned his attack for a takeover of the company at the annual stockholders' meeting scheduled for late May 1954. There was a major obstacle to his plan, though, and he would have to act fast.

Thwarted years earlier by the ICC in his first attempt to join NYC's board, because of his position at C&O, Young knew that he had to sever his connection with the company before he began his second attempt in earnest. He did so on January 19, 1954, relinquishing the C&O chairmanship to long-time ally and director, Cyrus Eaton. He was now freed from the legal encumbrances of his association with the C&O, and he lost no time maneuvering for control of NYC. He placed advertisements in the Wall Street Journal addressed to the stockholders of the New York Central soliciting nominations to the board of the company in anticipation of the annual meeting.

NYC countered with advertisements of its own. Popular magazines, such as *Life* and *Fortune,* as well as newspapers - some undoubtedly influenced by the Morgan interests - featured stories about the conflict. Some took up NYC's cause by taking direct aim at Young and his "record," with the help of an NYC publication called "What manner of man is Robert R. Young?" This publication, promulgated a month before the annual stockholders' meeting, painted an unflattering picture of Young, characterizing him as reckless with stockholders' money. It examined his tenure at C&O, highlighting his ill-fated *Chessie*, its three scrapped steam turbines, his acquisition of the Greenbrier Hotel, and taunted Young for his failure to produce his vaunted train of the future, referring to *Train X* as "still a figment of Mr. Young's imagination."

The war of words began a crescendo in January. Before long, the proxy battle became acrimonious, to the point where a tormented NYC President William White, in office just under two years, had to devote his full-time to the battle. In early June of 1954, when the vote was made official, Young's six year struggle resulted in his election as chairman of NYC's new board of directors—hand-picked by Young.

He now had a new forum for his projects. The railroad's passenger service was seriously ailing and Young realized that in order for NYC to be healthy he had to find effective solutions for its passenger service-related prob-

ARRIVING "FROM TOMORROW"
NEW YORK CENTRAL *Aerotrain*

The *Aerotrain* replaced the *Mercury* for a short time. It was a dramatic contrast to the train which had become twenty years before so popular. It is seen here at Chelsea, Michigan, eastbound.

lems. The stage was set for his *Train X*.

Young's proficiency as a financier, however, was not matched by his knowledge of detailed railroad operations. Consequently, he brought with him a 51-year old executive vice president from the Denver & Rio Grande Western to be NYC's president, Alfred Perlman. They met for the first time in May, 1954. In Perlman, Young found a kindred spirit for change who was endowed with both enthusiasm and a background in engineering and railroad operations.

Strangely enough, Young and Perlman were not a matched pair, philosophically. Whereas Young was a strident and unabashed proponent of passenger service, Perlman saw it as the industry's ruination.

Why, then, did Young choose Perlman to run his railroad? The answer seems to be found in the strengths and weaknesses of both men.

Young made no secret of the fact that he wasn't a railroad person—indeed, he saw this as one of his strengths. While he was an expert when it came to finances and he could charm his way through the most difficult of situations, he was lacking in detailed railway management and operational skills.

Perlman, however, embodied all the operational and technical talent which Young lacked. Reputedly personally abrasive, lacking tact and difficult to work with (and for), he was endowed with the breadth of railroad operational and engineering experience needed to lead NYC out of the perils which lay before it.

This is not to suggest that Young was easier to work for. He demanded much from his managers and was on occa-

sion given to expect more than might be considered "reasonable" - or even possible. Sometimes his optimism got the better of him.

In a conversation with his vice president of operations, Karl Borntrager, Young complimented him on being able to produce $52 million dollars in net revenue for 1955, but felt that it should have been $100 million dollars, since that was the amount the railroad earned in 1929! Young simply believed that there was no reason not to earn it again. Young went on to say that his *Train X*, which was about to make its debut, would "take care of that."[30]

Young did not have a high opinion of NYC's management, mostly former President White's people, although he allowed them to remain when he assumed control of the railroad. While remaining aloof, he drove the railroad's officials relentlessly (through Perlman) and did not mind telling them about their shortcomings when the railroad's performance failed to meet his expectations. Perlman did likewise.

It was an odd arrangement, but so long as Young could keep Perlman away from tampering with the passenger operations, they could co-exist. This, in fact, was their arrangement. So, Young had Perlman focus his attention on straightening out the railroad's beleaguered freight operation, while Young pursued *Train X*.[31]

Both NYC's freight and passenger operations were faltering badly. The situation was so critical, in fact, the railroad was on the precipice of entering bankruptcy - a detail that Young learned on the day after he took control of the railroad from William White.* That it would be avoided was due

* Railroad lawyers had actually drawn up the necessary documents under White's instructions.

Louis A. Marre

This view of *Xplorer* was taken before the NYC herald was applied to the pilot doors. The train consisted of one locomotive and nine cars, with a standard coupler behind the pilot doors for switching purposes—the engine had no other assignment. The train made a brief visit to Beech Grove Shops when this picture was taken on June 1, 1956.

to the combined efforts of Young and Perlman who managed to keep the company solvent. Perlman immediately got to work reorganizing operations, slashing the maintenance budget, and in improving the net returns from the freight business. Meanwhile, Young concentrated on maximizing the benefits of the railroad's extensive real estate holdings and directing that modest adjustments be made to the passenger operation to reduce costs and enhance revenues.

The typical NYC intercity passenger train in 1955 carried between 12 and 18 cars powered by two, and sometimes three, diesels. Trains of this size consisted of "headend" mail and express cars, coaches, and often dining and sleeper passenger cars, and required 7-10 man train crews. While many trains met their direct-train operating expenses, the overhead costs from station and terminal operations, to din-

ing and sleeping car operations—themselves further burdened with the heavy costs of excessive and unused capacity—created the overwhelming passenger deficits being realized by the company.

Under Young, a passenger research bureau was created and charged with the task of redesigning the railroad's passenger services while substantially reducing costs and increasing revenue. What emerged was NYC's "travel tailored schedules" concept, which called for a transition away from the railroad's traditional long-distance passenger train fleet in favor of more shorter passenger-only trains of five or six cars pulled by a single locomotive, designed to serve regional markets with fast schedules and five-man crews. Naturally, union labor was unenthusiastic about this proposal, as was the operating department which would have to

Van Dusen - Zillmer Collection
NYC's *Aerotrain* is arriving at South Bend, Indiana's Union Station on its run from Cleveland to Chicago in August 1956. In the background is the South Bend Studebaker plant. Studebaker shared *Aerotrain's* fate, but lasted longer.

Collection of Bert Pennypacker, Louis A. Marre Collection

Xplorer's engine was detachable from its train, a design feature which altered the train's ride. The mirrors and wind deflectors were added by NYC shop forces. The rear wheelset of the lead truck was equipped with General Railway Signal (GRS) train control - a standard NYC locomotive component. Cast NYC oval plates were applied to the *Xplorer's* flanks.

schedule freight trains over the same tracks.

This new plan narrowed the traditional NYC concept of the individual intercity passenger trains performing a variety of functions. It separated the mail and express function from the passenger business and intended to make the former a business in its own right by being handled as freight.

It also addressed the desirability of operating its passenger trains in fleets, one after the other across the system, often providing services which could be consolidated. Schedules were planned to permit more intensive use of equipment by reducing the number of cars and locomotives needed to provide the service.

The travel tailored concept took well over a year to develop and was expected to require a year to implement the system-wide changeover, in four installments, using schedule changes every three months. The first change

Glenn S. Moe, M. D. McCarter Collection

NYC's *Aerotrain* strikes a dramatic contrast to the depot during its scheduled stop in Niles, Michigan on May 6, 1956.

Xplorer is leaving Columbus, Ohio (westbound) in July 1956. In three hours it will be traversing the yard trackage of Cincinnati Union Terminal.

which took effect with the October 28, 1956 timetable, was developed with the cooperation of the various operating division superintendents and public officials in the states of New York, Massachusetts, Ohio, Indiana, and Michigan. The second change was to be implemented in February, 1957 and would focus on the west-end services operating between Chicago and Buffalo via Cleveland and Detroit.

With the October 1956 schedule, the railroad began to address the substantial costs of switching cars in and out of trains at intermediate stations. "Set-out" sleeping and dining cars were responsible for considerable costs, so a program of gradually phasing out the sleeping, dining car and intermediate "switch-out" and "switch-in" operations was initiated.

The stations were put up for sale at the same time - close to 400 of them. The high cost of maintenance alone justified their sale. Many saw this as evidence of Young's attempt to plunder the railroad's assets which only confirmed their belief that Young was a dangerous adventurer. In actuality, he and Perlman were taking a realistic approach to reducing the exorbitant passenger service overhead costs, including the enormous tax burden, while channeling the

assets into more productive uses.

In 1946, railroads held the distinction of being this country's primary intercity carrier of the traveling public. Ten years later, automobile traffic had eclipsed rail travel to the point where only 4.3% of intercity travel was by rail (88% was by automobile, 3.8% by bus, 3.4% by air).[32] The travel tailored schedules may have improved the railroad's passenger service, given time, but serious internal conflicts within Perlman's administration hampered its full implementation. As a result, many of the project's goals were never fully attained.

One of Young's avowed passions was presenting himself as the person who would revolutionize the rail passenger business, and he wanted to be characterized as being on the "cutting edge" of new ideas, as well as technology. Thus, he was not afraid to speak out and strike a blow against the government's policy of subsidizing the competition. His criticism, while valid, did not influence many in Congress, but he did manage to persuade some to examine, if not consider, his point of view.

One of those outside the railroad industry who saw the

rationale of Young's arguments about the regulatory atmosphere was ICC Chairman Richard R. Mitchell. On June 28, 1955, addressing the AAR Accounting Division meeting in Atlantic City, he agreed that it might be worthwhile for the government to subsidize rail passenger travel.

He stated, "We do not like the word 'subsidy.' Out in the middle west we don't use that word. We call it 'price support.' Why not call it 'passenger support?' If passenger trains are needed in the public interest, why shouldn't the public assist in carrying the cost instead of forcing upon the shippers of the nation the burden of paying the passenger deficit?"[33]

Naturally, Robert Young agreed. "We in the Central would rather give good service and be subsidized than to give poor service and be criticized by the passengers. Certainly, it would be better to have our competitors de-subsidized just as it would be better for all of us to be de-taxed! But so long as we are so prodigally tapped at the bunghole to build airways, waterways, and highways and terminals for our competitors, we in the Central, at least, are not too proud to welcome a little reciprocity at the barrel head."

He went on to say that, "... passenger and commuter service of the railroads, which have been rattling out at an accelerated pace for several decades, will crash on the dump heap within the next one unless the president's and Judge Mitchell's goal of equality of subsidy, taxation and regulation in transportation is realized."[34]

Of course, not everyone on the Commission was in agreement with Mitchell, but over time his observations would be acted upon on the local/state level and become integrated and accepted as part of transportation policy. Young's ideas did not escape the notice of those in influential positions.

Three years later, in more ominous tones, ICC hearings examiner Howard Hosmer would predict the demise of Pullman service by 1965—and the same fate for coach service by 1970.

With the battle for control of NYC behind him, Young resumed his campaign to implement change in the rail industry. He wasted no time in resurrecting his pursuit of the train of the future. NYC would be the stage upon which the eyes of the industry would be turned.

In 1955, Baldwin-Lima-Hamilton (B-L-H) received an order to begin production of the *Train X* diesel hydraulic locomotive, which was delivered to NYC in May 1956. Pullman-Standard received the orders for the nine cars—all coaches—in March 1955. Young had also persuaded another pro-passenger (albeit notorious) railroad president, Patrick McGinnis of neighboring New Haven Railroad, to order a twin set which became the *Daniel Webster.* NYC's *Train X* was then given a new name—*Xplorer.*

The Baldwin-built locomotive weighed 135,000 lbs. and was 11 feet high and 46 feet long. A single unit would power the train and contained an auxiliary 400-hp 6-cylinder diesel which would generate electricity for the train's lighting, heating and air conditioning systems. The locomotive employed the principle of "packaged maintenance," which afforded the railroad to remove the power plant in the locomotive after several thousand miles of operation so it could be quickly returned to service.[35]

P-S had done much of the preliminary design work in 1950 for the original *Train X* test car, so it was with little difficulty that it was able to begin construction of the coaches when it received the order from NYC, although there would be little resemblance between the test coach and those of *Xplorer.* The coaches would be built of aluminum and would consist of a center car, on each side of which were four articulated single-axle units of two cars each. The center car would be 50-1/2 feet long and would seat 40 passengers. The other cars would be 48 feet long and seat 48 passengers. The floor of the cars would be only 23 inches above the top of the rail.

One of the train's principal attributes was its ability to "lean" into curves at high speeds. This greatly improved the riding characteristics of the cars by allowing the passenger to remain at the same angle as when the train went along on straight track.

Each car would contain its own air conditioning system with power being drawn from the auxiliary power unit locat-

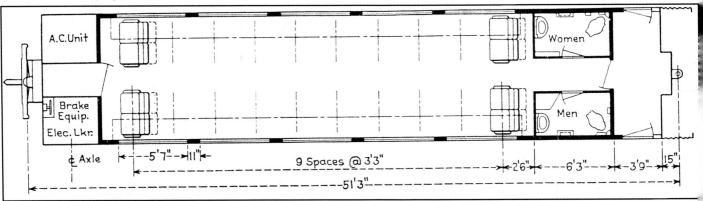

Railway Age

This is the floor plan for the 48-seat passenger, single-axle *Xplorer* coach.

ed in the locomotive. Forced hot air and electric convection units in each car would provide heat in winter months.

NYC began promoting the new trains in its 1956 timetables, even placing them on its System Form 1001 timetable covers. The railroad had high expectations and "hyped" the new services to the fullest in a fashion typical of the era. Meanwhile, NYC set to work on its image.

In one attempt to "soften" its otherwise austere image, the railroad altered its corporate insignia, the famous NYC oval. The "system" oval, in use since 1936, was immediately identifiable and one of the industry's most enduring corporate symbols. This was another idea of Thomas Deegan, whom Young had brought with him to NYC. Deegan felt that NYC's corporate symbol had to become more "friendly."

Beginning with the introduction of the *Xplorer*, the "Central" lettering was changed to script (quite similar to that of C&O's) and "system" replaced by horizontal lines. The emblem was used throughout NYC's advertising, timetables, and other publications, and began to appear on its passenger and some freight locomotives.

Xplorer's engine was painted in colors reminiscent of Young's former employer, C&O, in an attractive and distinctive scheme. Both locomotive and the cars featured cast aluminum NYC heralds of the new Deegan-inspired design, not decals, bolted onto the flanks of the train.

Aerotrain, meanwhile, was also all-aluminum decorated with a red stripe running the length of the train, tapered to a point on the locomotive. If nothing else, their appearance gained attention.

At the time of their promotion, Young was exclaiming that both *Xplorer* and the General Motors' designed and built *Aerotrain* (the latter was only temporarily in experimental service on NYC, see chapter 5) were not only new trains but heralded a new concept of improved "service." His argument struck a nerve for many in the pro-passenger press. The railroads' concept of "service" was slowly degenerating into "take it or leave it." Over time, discourteous service went undisciplined, further tarnishing the railroads' image, and was becoming commonplace.

Young would have none of this. Not only did he want to revitalize the passenger train, he wanted to restore its standards, while moving it to a profitable status.

Xplorer and *Aerotrain* were all-coach trains. Traditional dining service was expensive and did not fit into the "new train" economy concept. Food service revenues never even came close to meeting the expenses of a conventional dining car staffed with a crew of between seven and fifteen people. Maintenance of the dining car fleet pushed costs even higher. In lieu of a dining car, an innovation from airline operations and the Talgo was copied—tray meals would be served to each patron at his or her seat by "Cruisin' Susan." This practice resulted in mixed reviews.

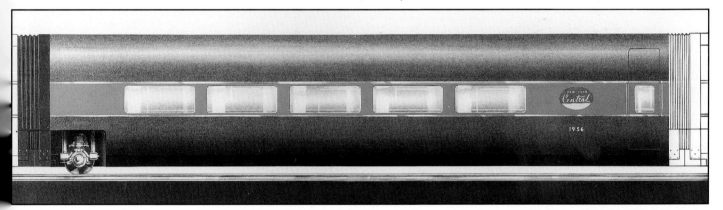

The artist rendering of the *Xplorer* coach.

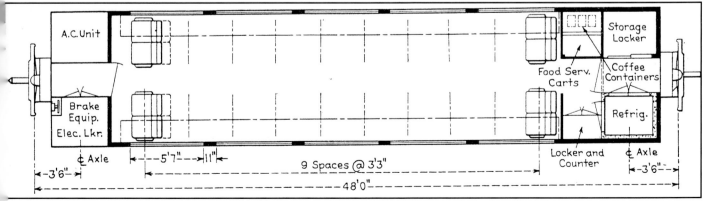

The floor plan of the food-dispensing end of the 40-seat passenger, two-axle *Xplorer* coach.

H. H. Harwood, Jr.

The rear of *Xplorer* seemed anticlimactic in comparison to its locomotive. The rear car is equipped with two couplers. The one in the doorway is an almost-standard AAR coupler used for switching purposes while the one below is for compatible *Xplorer* equipment. The whole train had to be turned at its destination, hence the need for the standard coupler. The train is seen leaving Wellington, Ohio in June 1956.

Both trains were sent around NYC's system on a promotional tour publicizing their inaugurations in a style reminiscent of the inauguration of the *Mercury* trains and the *20th Century Limited.* The railroad hadn't lost its touch for public relations.

Ceremonies for both trains included speeches by dignitaries and Young invited celebrities to ride the inaugural trips, among them a Miss America. *Aerotrain* was "launched" on January 5, 1956 in Chicago when it made a trip to Detroit for the benefit of the local press. The ceremonial event was even broadcast live over NBC Television's TODAY SHOW with Dave Garroway. In an interesting press release written in advance of the train's inaugural run, Deegan's office wrote, "Railroad men who were aboard hailed it as the beginning of a new era..." in a remarkable demonstration of public relations clairvoyance. The train used about $20 worth of fuel, according to Young—about one-quarter the amount for that of a regular train on the same run.

Aerotrain then toured the Santa Fe, Union Pacific, Southern Pacific, Illinois Central, Chicago & North Western, and Great Northern before entering service on NYC. The *Aerotrain* was first assigned a Chicago-Detroit run, departing from Illinois Central's 12th Street Station, beginning on April 29, 1956 before being switched to Chicago-Cleveland beginning in July.

Xplorer was inaugurated in ceremonies at both Cleveland and Cincinnati on May 16 and 17, 1956 respectively, and then went on display at Middletown and Dayton on May 18; Springfield on May 19; Columbus on May 20; and back to Cleveland for display on May 21. Originally scheduled to enter service on May 27, *Xplorer* was put on public display at New York City's Grand Central Terminal for two days which delayed its introduction as the *Ohio Xplorer.* It was assigned the Cleveland-Cincinnati corridor, replacing the southbound Mercury in the morning and offering a second northbound service in the afternoon, beginning revenue service on June 3, 1956. It remained in this service until it entered "commuter" service between Chicago and Elkhart, Indiana in 1957 and 1958 as trains Nos. 741 and 210.

The Cleveland-Cincinnati route was chosen by passenger traffic department because of the institution of experimental fares on that portion of the railroad and also because

passenger traffic on the run between Cleveland and Cincinnati had been showing "small but steady increases between most points during the year 1955." Beginning in January 1956, however, a decline in passenger traffic developed in all the markets except between Cleveland and Columbus, where the railroad experienced a slight increase in traffic.[36]

Patrons and rail officials alike suddenly encountered a serious drawback to the trains. Their rides were anything but smooth and quiet. NYC gave *Xplorer* and *Aerotrain's* passengers "report cards" to help evaluate public reaction to the trains. While they gave *Aerotrain* high points for its air conditioning and modern appeal, its riding quality suffered and passengers stressed that it needed improvement. *Xplorer's* patrons expressed similar sentiments in their polls.

Aside from *Xplorer's* poor riding qualities, however, reports were not all negative. While the interior designs differed from conventional coaches, most riders gave the train favorable responses in regard to seat comfort. And while after decades of eating finely prepared meals in an atmosphere of elegance inside a conventional dining car, one would think that eating a tray meal at one's seat (even if it was delivered by "Cruisin' Susan") would be an exercise in "culture shock." Surprisingly, however, passenger research revealed that it was rare for more than 10-20% of coach travelers on shorter trips to eat in the diner and most, 72.4% of those surveyed, gave the Cruisin' Susan food service a favorable rating.[37] The food service cart gave the seats a beating, though.

Xplorer was plagued with other problems, however. While GM's *Aerotrain* was powered by a 1200 hp Model 567 diesel engine with electric drive, one of the most reliable products GM ever made, the Baldwin locomotive was powered by a 1000 hp Maybach V-12, MD-655 diesel engine which powered a four-speed hydraulic transmission (called "Mechydro") which developed trouble when it tried to shift into its high-speed mode, causing its engine to over-heat and shut down. The transmission was not unlike that of an automobile. Each of its four speed ranges had limits to 26, 43, 70 and 120 mph that when reached necessitated shifting to a higher gear. Even more problems were experienced in its electrical control apparatus and piping. Although the locomotive was available 93.2% of the time in a 147 day period

between June and October 1956, the balance during the same period was spent in the Collinwood Shop being repaired.[38] And when the engine failed en route, it required assistance from conventional locomotives, which only further damaged *Xplorer's* credibility.

Another negative factor which hurt the project was the traditional approach in which the train was maintained. This aspect alone presented a host of complications. As with *The Comet,* when one car had to be serviced, the whole train was taken out of service. Unlike the Burlington Route, which built a separate and dedicated facility for the servicing of its famous articulated *Zephyr* trains, NYC did not have a special facility to maintain a train of such sophisticated construction and relied upon conventional shop layouts for the train's maintenance.

So, a clash between the traditional and the future suddenly manifested itself. The mechanical staff at Collinwood, responsible for the maintenance and repair of *Xplorer,* was unfamiliar with the new designs and was inadequately trained. After *Xplorer* arrived, NYC mechanical forces had to pay constant attention to the train because of its unique features. Sometimes they were ill-prepared to deal with the locomotive's idiosyncrasies, its metric-sized fittings, bolts, nuts, etc. While the hydraulic transmission was widely used in Europe, it was a novelty in the U. S. and NYC's mechanical department was unfamiliar with its servicing and repair. This was a fateful shortcoming. Familiar only with existing conventional equipment, the railroad's maintenance crews applied traditional solutions which were not best-suited for a train of a totally new design. Complicating matters further, spare parts were not readily available. Then there were the design changes which created problems.

One of the alterations from the original *Train X* design and the *Xplorer* was that the initial concept called for a locomotive at both ends of the train. NYC, in a cost cutting move, eliminated one engine from the train's consist which underpowered the train, and made it necessary to turn the train for the return trip which was both difficult and very expensive. This also created a destabilized suspension system contributing to the train's uneven ride, especially near the end of the train. As a result, trainmen were instructed to place all passengers in the forward cars, if at all possible, and only when those cars were filled were they to seat anyone in the rear cars.

Another change in the original design altered the articulation of the locomotive and the cars. NYC's mechanical department wanted the freedom to replace the locomotive (so it could go to the engine house for fueling and maintenance while the cars went to the coach yard for cleaning and servicing), so it became an independent unit. At higher speeds this non-articulated arrangement destabilized the forward end of the first coach producing a galloping effect.

When the *Train X* design plans arrived in NYC's

mechanical engineering office, details of the designs for the cars' suspension were altered with the intention of making improvements. The cars' overhead suspension was originally designed by Alan Cripe and placed in the C&O prototype car, but NYC's mechanical engineers (and those at P-S) chose to replace it with a more traditional supportive system for ease of maintenance. This change dramatically altered the ride of the train.

Because the air suspension of the cars was of a bellows-type fed from the train's air line, engineers were instructed not to allow the air pressure on the brake pipe to drop below 90 pounds. Normal operating pressure was between 110 -120 pounds. If the pressure were to drop below 90 pounds, the air suspension on the cars would collapse (prompting train crews to nickname the train "Xploder"), such as when the train was placed in "emergency."[39] This deficiency could have been overcome with little effort, but it wasn't a priority.[40]

In addition, while locomotive engineers were thoroughly versed in the train's operation, they were not familiar with how to fix minor problems, although an instruction manual was chained to the control stand in the locomotive for reference. Unfortunately, the manual for the diesel hydraulic was printed in German.[41]

There were other deterrents. The "new trains" would be handicapped severely if the existing rate structure did not entice and encourage riding them. The fares had to be perceived as economical, but the rate structure was inflexible by design.

Transit times were not improved because of existing speed restrictions and operating conservatism - a provision that would enable conventional equipment to operate on the same schedules. Welded rail would not be installed across NYC for another ten years, and while Xplorer's ride was smoother and quieter than Aerotrain's, it was rough at slow speeds, especially in terminal areas. The train's speed would have to increase if it were to compete with the automobile.

It should be mentioned that in many cases the technical problems which these trains experienced were overcome. The Xplorer's difficulties with the hydraulic transmission were not insoluble and were corrected. In a report on Xplorer's performance by the passenger research department, the train was given a 91.8% availability record for the 147 day period June 3 to October 27, 1956. Unfor-tunately, by the time the

Pier Clifford, H. H. Harwood, Jr. Collection

The ends of the *Xplorer* coaches were a study in "function." Visible is the receptacle end of the coupling with the electrical connections on either side at top. *Aerotrain's* couplings were similar in design. Over the doorway is the train's main power train-line. The "pony" trucks were lowered when the cars were separated. The photo was taken at Columbus, Ohio during the train's demonstration tour.

mechanical difficulties were ameliorated, the train's other faults and the economic factors combined to kill the project.

There were other factors, not so well known, that also led to the failure of NYC's lightweight train experiments. Not everyone at NYC was enthusiastic about the Xplorer or about reviving the passenger business. Robert Young not only had to convince the public of his ideas and vision, he had his own administration to contend with, and they often worked at cross-purposes.

While outwardly supportive (because of his boss), Alfred Perlman saw no value in rail passenger service and viewed the lightweight experiments as a waste of time and expense

Collection of Lloyd D. Lewis, TLC Collection

New Haven's *Daniel Webster* was *Xplorer*'s non-identical twin. The engine's exterior was slightly different in the nose design, and there were subtle differences inside the coaches. The paint scheme was as different as the railroad could manage. It shared *Xplorer*'s fate. It is seen at New Haven shortly after delivery in late 1956.

Not surprisingly, his operating people were unenthusiastic about the projects and while they may not have obstructed the experiments, they did not go out of their way to help them. To Perlman's operating people, passenger trains were a nuisance—they got in the way of their freight trains.

In 1956, half of NYC's train-miles—but less than 10% of its car-miles—were in passenger service, which on average produced only 25% of the revenue generated by the freight train-miles. Perlman saw this as a squandering of precious assets. To Perlman, the trains of the future meant high speed freight trains.

There were other internal conflicts at NYC. The railroad actually had two passenger departments. The most visible was the department of passenger sales and services, headed by Vice President Ernest C. Nickerson; the other was less visible and buried within the accounting department but with a direct line to Alfred Perlman, who gave it his principal attention.[42] Meanwhile, Young remained aloof from the departmental infighting.

In the end, GM's adaptation of the bus design was not successful and in the latter part of October 1956, *Aerotrain* 1001 was returned to GM. The *Xplorer* was eventually stored, then sold in December 1960 to the Pickens Railroad in South Carolina. NYC's lightweight train experiment was over—not so the concept of the train of the future, however.

While Young met a violent and tragic end in late January 1958, his legacy resurfaced in July 1966 when NYC "experi-

My First Encounter with the Xplorer

*by Fred "Brownie" Markley,
Retired Big Four Engineer*

"I guess I was always prejudiced against the *Xplorer*. My first view of it was embarrassing—I was on a local freight, the Valley Run at Middletown. We were eastbound. As we were getting the air released on our train, I ran over to a trackside Dairy Queen. The girl working there asked me when "that new train" was coming through.

I said that I didn't know. Well, as we pulled out of Middletown, this was before radio, the conductor set the air when we cleared the yard switch and gave us a "back up" signal with a fusee. We had something over 100 cars which meant that in order to clear the main line, we had to back into a coal yard at the west end of the siding.

To make a long story short, I stopped about two feet too soon, then had to release the brakes and shove back to get over the derail so that the main track switch could be lined for the *Xplorer*.

For what seemed an eternity, I had to look down into the cab of the *Xplorer* which was filled with 'white shirts and ties.' I think everybody from the general manager on down was on that train."

NYC's M497 rockets through Bryan, Ohio during tests in July 1966. The purpose of the tests was to determine the effects and feasibility of high-speed trains on existing rail components. NYC claimed that the future of passenger service lay in the concept of high-speed, short-haul service. The likes of M497 as witnessed here have not been seen since.

J. W. Swanberg

New Haven's *Daniel Webster* locomotives differed from *Xplorer's* not only in their appearance. They contained an additional electrical system which allowed them to use NYC's third-rail d.c. power to gain access to Grand Central Terminal. With a locomotive on both ends, like the *Comet*, the *Daniel Webster* enters Hartford on March 5, 1958.

mented" with another concept, also with mixed results. This time the "train" would be called, "The Pride of the Central," even if its creators had little intention of placing it in service.

NYC's "Pride" was a Budd rail diesel car (RDC) M497, fitted with two jet engines mounted on the roof, a menacing-looking cowl with two windows (actually number board covers from an EMD freight engine) and a disconnected drive shaft. There is some debate about what this supersonic RDC was to demonstrate. NYC stated that the experiment was intended to test and document the effect of high-speed transport over existing rail systems to ascertain the viability of high-speed passenger rail transport of the future.

Another explanation, perhaps closer to the truth, was that NYC was trying to enhance its position during the on-going Penn Central merger negotiations. The Pennsylvania Railroad was then experimenting with high-speed trains in its Northeast Corridor between New York and Washington and spending millions of (government) dollars in the process. NYC's budget for its project was limited to $35,000. The car made four runs over a two day period, on July 23 and 24, 1966, east of Butler, Indiana. Some felt that NYC's purpose was not to demonstrate what high-speed rail could be, but rather what it was not. Here was the fastest "train" on rails and it couldn't take the curves at high speeds. Existing technology did not yet allow for truly high-speed rail in this country.

At the time that this experiment was taking place, NYC's passenger service was a pale shadow of what it had been ten years earlier when it had experimented with another version of the train of the future. By this time the railroads desperately wanted to get out of the passenger business. While some had succeeded, NYC was still operating passenger trains in the face of declining passenger usage, declining revenues and rising losses. Obviously, it had no intention of instituting the type of train it sent screaming along its mainline in northern Ohio.

Proponents of rail service stated that its future lay in short-haul, high-speed intercity trains, even though the necessary technology was not highly developed in this country, unlike in Europe and Japan.

Certainly, there were a lot of politics involved. Others felt that the experiment was meant to silence the critics of the railroad who were saying that the railroads weren't doing enough to examine high-speed rail. Whether or not this was in fact the case remains a subject for debate. What is known is that after the high-speed runs were made, where the car obtained a top speed of 183.85 mph, the jet engines and cowling were removed, and the M497 was parked on a siding.

Within the next four years, passenger service on the

J. W. Swanberg Collection

"A cross between Darth Vader and Jet Jackson" is how the author described NYC's RDC-2 M497 parading as the "Pride of the Central." The jet-powered car reached a top speed of 183.85 mph in four tests. After the tests were made, the car was parked on a siding and was eventually scrapped.

High-Speed Project

Excerpted from the 1967 Penn Central Annual Report

Penn Central's 226-mile main line between New York and Washington has been upgraded into the best roadway in the world in preparation for high-speed passenger service. Welded rail, new ties and ballast, high-level station platforms, stronger catenary wire and other improvements have been made. Inauguration of the service awaits delivery and acceptance of a fleet of 50 self-propelled Metroliner passenger cars being built by the Budd Company.

Penn Central is investing $45 million and the United States Department of Transportation $11 million in this demonstration project to test public acceptance of an entirely new type of rail travel.

The Metroliner fleet will cost more than $21 million and emphasizes speed, convenience, safety and luxury. The cars are highly complicated vehicles, far advanced in design and much more powerful than any passenger equipment previously built in this country.

nation's railroads was driven to the brink of extinction before the Federal Government stepped in to create Amtrak. Congress saw in the Northeast Corridor the potential for high-speed rail service - similar in theory, if not in mechanical design, to the ideas of Robert Young.

In the contemporary world, Amtrak has experimented with newly designed Talgo and European ICE trains and sent them around the country much in the same way that the *Aerotrain* was toured in the 1950s. Whether they will meet a similar fate depends upon the success of their designers in producing a comfortable high-speed train that can operate on existing (often rough) tracks in harmony with heavy freight trains. It will also depend upon the public's desire to use the new services, the courage and ability of the nation's political leaders to invest in its future, and their willingness to allow the passenger rail services to grow.

A Ride On The Xplorer

by Paul J. Friedlander

CINCINNATI - *Train X,* one of the mystic weapons by Robert R. Young when he came riding out of the Midwestern realm of the Chesapeake & Ohio Railroad to take over control of the New York Central, appeared on the rails last week actually carrying passengers. Most appropriately, the demonstration of the new design, light-weight, low-slung train was made between Cleveland and Cincinnati. This is the run where *Train X,* or the *Xplorer* as it is now known, will start carrying paying passengers next Sunday, and it is also the heartland of the C&O.

The *Xplorer* started in 1947 as a gleam in Mr. Young's eye when he was chairman of the board of the C&O. Much of the preliminary design work was done by C&O men on C&O drafting tables, and some of them moved out to stay with the job as it was finally done by the New York Central, Pullman-Standard, which built the coaches, and Baldwin-Lima-Hamilton which built the Diesel engine under license from German railroad patents.

So much time has elapsed between *Train X's* first blueprints and the christening ceremony, with champagne, in the Cleveland terminal, that it must be put into its historical perspective before we consider its relative merits:

1950 - ACF Industries built a *Talgo* articulated lightweight train for the Spanish national railway, which has been using the train happily, safely and economically ever since.

1951 - Pullman-Standard built an experimental car for Train X and started track tests.

1955 - General Motors unveiled its *Aerotrain,* an articulated high-speed train based on GM bus designs.

1956 - January: New York Central and Pennsylvania Railroads each took delivery of a GM *Aerotrain* and put them into regular passenger service on a test basis. February: The Rock Island Railroad received a *Talgo* train from ACF and started running it between Chicago and Peoria.

More Trains Coming

And now the *Xplorer,* and next month the Budd Company will show its tubular train, reportedly a train midway between the heavy standard equipment and the extremely lightweight new ones. The Santa Fe is already exhibiting its high-level car, a standard-weight train with the passengers all seated upstairs for a quieter ride and greater

J. Parker Lamb

The eastbound *Xplorer* is just north of Fairborn, Ohio in the spring of 1957. The lower numbers, such as No. 20, were reserved for experimental projects. One of the reasons for its failure was that the train was rushed into service without adequate testing and breaking in. Once the "bugs" were worked out, the Baldwin-assembled locomotive ran quite well, but by then it was too late.

visibility.

Obviously, for the American railroads this is a time of uncertainty and for shopping around for new equipment. They are searching for trains that will be light in weight, therefore cheaper to build, cheaper to haul, and will require less expensive right of way and track maintenance. The idea is to make money for the roads by cutting initial investments and operating costs, and by winning back from private automobiles, the bus lines and the airlines the short-haul (under 500 miles) passenger.

The *Xplorer* is said to be the lightest train in the field—700 pounds per passenger. Without the locomotive, its 392 seats work out to $1,650 each, against a $2,850 per seat cost in conventional coaches. What the railroad directors seek is a train costing $1 per pound, which is roughly what a plain automobile costs (exclusive of dealer discounts) when you get above the Ford, Chevrolet and Plymouth price levels.

Among themselves, railroad officials agree that none of the new trains—Talgo, *Aerotrain*, *Xplorer*—are the complete answer. Speaking as one who has tried them all, this passenger agrees heartily. When they were planning these trains, the engineers hoped to provide a ride as smooth, as fast but less noisy, and with almost the same feeling of solidity and stability as the heavy new trains give. They have not been able to do it so far, and although they argue that these new trains are early prototypes subject to improvement, at this stage it does not look as if they can achieve their goal.

Weight for Comfort

A heavy automobile gives a smoother ride than a light car; a big, heavy airplane has more stability than a light plane; a big ship rides steadier than a small one. It seems logical that a good, new heavy train will run more comfortably than

During a station stop at Columbus, Ohio the conductor and assistant conductor confer with the train's female attendant. One must presume that the lady is the well-publicized "Cruisin' Susan."

H. H. Harwood, Jr.

The nine car eastbound *Xplorer* slows to stop at Wellington, Ohio in June 1956. Going by train was still an elegant way to travel as evidenced by the lady at left.

a train only one-third as heavy.

Furthermore, the way the roads are using the new experimental train is proof of their changing thoughts. The Pennsylvania runs its *Aerotrain* 439.3 miles, New York to Pittsburgh, making a complete round trip each day. The Central has its *Aerotrain* doing 283.5 miles between Chicago and Detroit, and the *Xplorer* will cover 257.8 miles between Cleveland and Cincinnati.

These are short trips, with many stops where the fast deceleration and acceleration of the lightweight trains save time and money. The passengers, getting on and off at the many way stations, are rarely on the train for more than five or six hours. If the roads ever get around to offering competitive rate reductions for these streamlines runs, they will very likely pull a lot of passengers out of automobiles and busses and off some local airline flights.

Superficially, all the new underslung trains look alike. Their picture windows, airplane type reclining seats, gay interiors using synthetics for bright colors and easy cleaning, give the passenger all the makings for a happy trip. There is no

diner; food service is from rolling carts, called on the *Xplorer* "Cruisin' Susans."

The casual passenger would be hard put to tell whether he is aboard a Talgo, an *Aerotrain* or the *Xplorer*. They all look and ride pretty much alike. This comparison shopper puts the *Xplorer* at the top of the three for its soundproofing. Pullman-Standard poured all kinds of insulating material into its car bodies, built the bodies in two shells—one hung inside the other on rubber—and thus reduced the noise level to acceptable standards.

Riding on Air

The *Xplorer* combined the best features of the suspension systems of the Talgo and *Aerotrain* using a compressed air spring plus snubbers and side struts that swing the train very smoothly into the sharpest of curves at high speeds. It also uses only two wheels on a single axle at the end of each car, the other wheel-less end resting on the rear end of the car ahead.

The *Xplorer* has less noise, rattle and rock and roll than did the original *Aerotrain*s. Some lengthwise jiggling developed on the press run, but this, the engineers promised, will be fixed before next Sunday. Because of track speed limits, the train did not exceed 79 miles per hour, and this train, too, as in the other lightweights, the higher speeds proved much smoother than low speeds.

The three new trains have a tendency to vibrate uneasily at low speeds.

In all three trains, the front-most cars ride best. The Talgo has a peculiar characteristic—when it gets above 70 miles an hour you can almost feel the train stretch out like a greyhound after a stuffed rabbit, taking off down the track with a smooth, solid sensation of comfortable speed. Neither the *Aerotrain* nor the *Xplorer* now match this, but for riding quality the *Xplorer* takes second place easily over the GM entry.

Compromise

While the *Xplorer* doesn't suffer from side-slap, like the other two, it is so light that its two-wheel axles bounce over rough track joints, switch points and other track crossings. The original ride was a bit soft, jiggling frequently—more like a bus than a train. This too the engineers promise to remedy simply by increasing the pressure in the pneumatic suspension system.

To do this they will have to compromise between a comfortable ride at high speeds, requiring softer suspension, and a comfortable ride at low speeds, which needs the harder suspension. Apparently in railroading, as in other things, you cannot have it both ways at once.

Where the *Xplorer* has every other train on the tracks beaten—both the big ones and the new little ones—is in the space it has allocated to its lavatories. Instead of telephone-booth cubicles, these are spacious quarters with room to turn around in. Other railroads, and especially the airlines, please copy.

Railroads are especially interested in the German engine built for the *Xplorer*. It is only a 1,000-horsepower Diesel, not powerful enough to handle the *Xplorer* as easily with as fast acceleration as the railroads want. (A big, fast American passenger train uses enough Diesel-electric units to give it 4,000 horsepower.)

But the *Xplorer* engine is being built in a larger, more powerful size which should do the job satisfactorily. And its great virtue is that it is not a Diesel-electric, as are the locomotives used on most American railroads, but simply a Diesel.

In the diesel-electric engine, the oil-burning Diesel does not drive the train. It drives generators which produce electricity to drive the electric motors that turn the train wheels. The *Xplorer*'s Diesel drives the locomotive wheels directly through an automatic transmission and direct drive shaft.

The automatic transmission is described by those who should know as a kind of combination of the Hydramatic and the Dynaflow torque converter transmissions. the engineman has a shift lever that goes to forward, reverse and neutral. He has an airbrake lever, and the only other thing he uses to run the train, outside the whistle, is a throttle with six positions.

Six-Notch Throttle

He puts the gear shift into forward or reverse, and then shoves the throttle through the six positions to top speed. The oil-coupled transmission does the rest, shifting automatically through speeds as its load permits. At 65 miles an hour, the mechanism jumps into top drive, or high gear.

The German inventors and the German railways report great success with this power source and transmission. It eliminates the generators and complicated wiring required in a Diesel-electric locomotive, thereby reducing the amount of machinery and odds and ends that can wear out and need replacement. This cuts maintenance costs and reduces even further the comparatively small time the Diesel-electrics have to spend unproductively in shops. The transmission apparently is sturdy enough to stand up under the work loads in hauling freight trains across Germany's mountain tracks.

The *Xplorer* locomotive has, right behind its big Diesel engine, a smaller one that spins a generator to furnish electricity for the train lights and to run its heating and air-conditioning apparatus.

The New York, New Haven and Hartford Railroad has an *Xplorer* on order with a Diesel engine on each end. This will permit the line to reverse the seats when the train stops at Grand Central Terminal, take on a new load of passengers and run the train right out again without the costly turning-around operation.

It's A Tough Job

Incidentally, a ride in the *Xplorer* cab makes one wonder why any American youth in his right mind wants to be a train engineer. It is a much more frightening experience than looking over the shoulder of an airplane pilot. The latter has seemingly, the whole sky and an unlimited number of dimensions in which to maneuver.

The engineer has only one place to go—straight down the tracks. With the automatic signal systems and good track this sounds fine, until you run through highly populated Ohio. Then you realize that the poor engineer is at the mercy of motorists at every crossing he passes.

The crossing lights flash and the whistle blows long and penetratingly but the truck and passenger car drivers insist on pushing the noses of their vehicles almost on the tracks. The engineer sits there, outwardly calm as a Buddha in overalls and the train drives down over the crossing with what, to the inexperienced eye, seems less than inches to spare. I saw enough, but it is also enough to turn one's hair gray and turn one quickly back to the comforting calm of a steward bearing liquid sedation.

Epilogue

"The railroads have not left the passengers, the passengers have left the railroads."

- Stuart K. Saunders, chairman,
Pennsylvania Railroad 1966

On January 25, 1958, a deeply troubled Robert R. Young ended his life with a shotgun blast in the billiard room of his Palm Beach, Florida home just a few weeks short of his 61st birthday.

William R. White left NYC to become president, and later chairman, of Delaware & Hudson Railway (1954-1966), and concurrently with ICC approval, chairman of Erie-Lackawanna from 1963 to the day of his death, April 6, 1967. He was 70.

Thomas Deegan left NYC very shortly after Young's death and went on to head the 1964-65 New York World's Fair. He died in November 1977 at the age of 67.

Alfred Perlman became chairman of the board after Young's death and in 1968 became Penn Central's first president. He died on April 30, 1983.

Kenneth Browne retired from C&O to live in Lexington, Virginia where he died on November 26, 1985 at the age of 80.

Alan Cripe went on to develop United Aircraft's Turbotrain, and his yet-to-be built "Fastracker" diesel and turbine-powered motor trains, which used many of Xplorer's design principles. He died at age 70 on December 15, 1994.

New York Central and the Pennsylvania were merged to become Penn Central on February 1, 1968 and became the largest bankrupt railroad in history soon thereafter. It evolved into Conrail in April 1976 and by the last decade of the century it was transformed into one of the most prosperous railroads in the country, only to become the object of corporate lust.

The Chesapeake and Ohio Railway was absorbed by its parent, CSX, in September 1987 to become a part of CSX Transportation. In 1997 it bought and absorbed almost half of Conrail.

The Alleghany survives as a corporation specializing in insurance, title, property, and financial services.

ACF stopped building passenger cars in 1961. It still exists today as a builder of freight cars.

Pullman-Standard built its last passenger car in 1981 (for Amtrak) when too few orders and cost overruns made building passenger cars unprofitable.

Baldwin-Lima-Hamilton, conceived in response to competition, succumbed to the dominance of GM and General Electric in October 1956. The *Xplorer* diesel hydraulic locomotive was to be among its last products.

The *Xplorers* left NYC and the Pennsylvania Railroad (which extended its lease of the train to June 30, 1957) and subsequently were bought by the Rock Island, which used them in commuter service for ten years before donating them to the National Transportation Museums in St. Louis, Missouri and in Green Bay, Wisconsin. (Note: *Xplorer* 1000 ran on Canadian National during 1957, before being sold to the Rock Island for Chicago-Joliet service in October, 1958; *Xplorer* 1001 ran on the Union Pacific Railroad as its *City of Las Vegas* from December, 1956 to September, 1957, then operated on the Santa Fe, Rock Island, Southern Pacific, and in Mexico, before being sold to the Rock Island in October, 1958.)

Xplorer was sold to James F. Jones, president of the Pickens Railroad (as was New Haven's *Daniel Webster*) in May 1960 and was used in tourist excursion service. In 1963 it was used in tests by United Aircraft during the development of its Turbotrain. It was then returned to the Pickens Railroad, but as systems broke down and were too difficult and expensive to be repaired, it was parked on a siding in Travelers Rest, South Carolina.

Passenger Service

Excerpted from the 1967 Penn Central Annual Report

Penn Central is promoting a new role for rail passenger service in the future transportation system of an urbanized America. It is based on the concept that commuter and limited intercity rail passenger systems are a public service which must have public support. It will concentrate on development of improved equipment and facilities for commuters in metropolitan areas and the introduction of high-speed, luxury, intercity travel over intermediate distances.

Concurrently, we are under taking a far-reaching program for adjusting our present service to actual public needs. We will proceed to phase out long-haul passenger runs and other service which the public has demonstrated it neither wants nor needs. During the past year, the Twentieth Century Limited between New York and Chicago was discontinued and two other trains between these cities, the Broadway Limited and The General, were combined.

Our passenger deficit in 1967 rose to $85 million, up 38% above the $61.4 million of 1966. A decline in passenger volume, mounting wage and benefit costs, and curtailment of mail shipments contributed to this loss. Passenger revenues in 1967 dropped 11.4%, to $115 million.

(Note: This is a combined report for both New York Central and Pennsylvania Railroads.)

Both *Xplorer* and *Daniel Webster* were scrapped in the early 1970s.

The reasons for the failure of both *Train X* and the *Xplorer* went beyond their mechanical shortcomings. Young believed that among the fundamental reasons why the passenger train business was faltering, aside from government, banking and union interference, was that the railroads themselves weren't paying attention to the market, i.e. doing enough to promote rail travel and were not being responsive in their approach to the public. While he felt that the technology had to change, railroad management and public regulation had to keep pace in order for the industry to remain competitive. Furthermore, the railroads' urge to get out of the passenger business far exceeded their desire to stay in it.

But, if Young's *Train X* failed to meet his expectations and was truly a "failure," then what of his other goals related to passenger service, such as the potential for its profitability? Was it simply unrealistic to believe that passenger service could become profitable? The railroads thought so - they had decades of passenger deficits to prove their case. While Young was certainly bucking the tide of industry consensus relating to rail passenger service, he was not alone in his belief that it was possible to operate passenger service at a profit.

In a report sponsored by the Railway Progress Institute (RPI) titled "Passengers and Profits - An Economic Study of the Earning Potential of Railroad Passenger Services," based on fiscal year 1955, many of Young's theories about existing passenger service and its potential were effectively supported in its conclusions. Dated March 1959 and prepared for the Committee on Passenger Traffic Research of RPI by Transportation Facts, Inc., it was boldly stamped "CONFIDENTIAL - Not For Publication." The timing of the report seems to suggest that others who had a stake in the survival of rail passenger service, such as the industry suppliers who made up RPI, were influenced by Young's message of optimism, enough so to authorize a lengthy and qualitative study on the issue. The fact that it was issued in 1959 (three years after the deficit hearings in Washington and after the indus-

try had begun to concentrate its efforts on passenger service elimination), but never published, seems to support those who feel that the report was suppressed by the AAR. By that time, government was finally showing signs of sympathy for the railroads' position. The last thing the railroads wanted was a report which ran counter to their efforts and which demonstrated that the railroads could, in fact, earn profits running passenger trains.

The in-depth study examined and compared the aspects of travel trends between rail, bus and air, including vehicle speed and occupancy; marketing; labor, operating, maintenance, facility, and equipment costs; as well as the cost effects of government regulation, union contractual arrangements, geographical aspects and inefficiency, to name but a few. Many of its incidental conclusions regarding high costs supported those of the railroads, but its overall conclusions were at variance with those of the industry.

It found, for example, that a comparison of labor costs between the train and the bus was heavily weighted in favor of the bus. It vividly stated the obvious, while illustrating the disparity between them, which was not so obvious.

"At present 100 miles of travel is considered a day's work for locomotive engineers and firemen. For trainmen, 150 miles is the rule. These rules often enable a train crew to collect a full day's wages for two or three hours' work.

How much do these and other rules inflate operating costs? And, what would it cost to operate passenger train service if only necessary crews were used and worked seven hours a day in 'en-route' duty?

In 1955, 299 million train-miles were operated with 7,513,000 'train-hours' at about 40 miles per hour. Crew costs were $105 million for enginemen and $140.7 million for trainmen, or a total cost of $245.7 million. This figure reduces to a cost of $.82 per train-mile, or $32.70 per train-hour.

Corresponding bus-industry data is as follows: 861.4 million bus-miles were operated at an estimated average speed of 30 miles per hour (28.7 million 'bus-hours'). Driver expenses of $82 million equate to $.095 per bus-mile or $2.86 per hour."[43]

Passenger Services: A New Study

Excerpted from the 1966 NYC Annual Report

Central's passenger deficit during 1966 was slightly over $16 million. Strikes on the New York City subways in January and on the nation's airlines during July and August resulted in short-term increases in passenger volume. The continuing deficit, however, reflects an overall reduction in intercity sleeping car and long-haul coach traffic, as well as the added costs of further wage increases.

During the year, a marketing study was started to determine how to restructure the Company's passenger operations, other than suburban, to meet modern travel needs. The study found that, according to a 1963 Bureau of Census survey of travel patterns, 74% of all trips in the nation were for distances of under 200 miles.

Central's operations, on the other hand, are not geared to serve this dominate passenger market. Instead, our trains now cater to a rapidly diminishing number of travelers who use overnight dining, sleeping, and baggage car services for longer distances — at tremendous overhead cost to the railroad.

Our study to date indicates that there may be a greater demand for a shuttle-type service which will permit comfortable high-speed travel within the 200-mile range. We are continuing to analyze the potential market for this type of service.

Wm. A. Swartz, M. D. McCarter Collection

Aerotrain No. 1 (C.R.I.P.) was scrapped in the mid 1960s. No. 1000 (ex-PRR) became R.I. No. 2 and was retired to the National Transportation Museum in Green Bay, Wisconsin. No.1001 (ex-NYC, et al) became R.I. No. 3 and was retired to the National Transportation Museum in St. Louis, Missouri. October 19, 1967.

While this was hardly a surprise, the report continued by questioning if staffing of four or five train crew members was really necessary. It addressed the issue of break even costs and came to the conclusion that the factors which controlled the existing deficiency in railroad car-mile revenues were insufficient capacity operated and the insufficient percent of seats sold. The load factor needed to break even in a coach was 39.4%; in a sleeper, 67.9%. The report concluded that "if a percentage of seats comparable to [bus] competition were occupied, then a net rail coach rate of only 2 cents would produce 80 cents per car-mile - more than enough for profits."[44]

Rail load factors being realized were 32.8% in coach and 41.2% in first class. The report concluded by adding that profits "far in excess of those enjoyed by Class I buses or the domestic trunk airlines could be achieved in intercity rail passenger operations," given adequate equipment utilization.[45]

When compared with the bus and airplane, the passenger train fared poorly in equipment utilization. The report cited a DC-6 and a Constellation being in the air 8 out of 10 hours a day with 70% capacity, whereas the average rail passenger car was in service but 5 hours a day at 33% capacity. Meanwhile, the bus operated at 60% capacity for 9 to 10 hours each day. The report concluded that the average airline and bus seats were used 6 to 7 hours a day by a customer, while the rail coach seat was filled only 2 to 3 hours a day, or about 1/3 that of the competition.*

While comparative airline costs were high, the fact that the airlines enjoyed a greater occupancy rate per passenger-mile produced greater revenues. So, while airplanes filled 70% of their seats, and the railroads 30-35%, resulting costs were $3.84 for planes and $2.43 to $2.83 for the rail coach; but, the average revenue produced per passenger-mile was $4.32 for the airline and $2.47 for the rail carriers. The conclusion was that if rail service could be operated with the same occupancy rate as the airplane, rail fares could be reduced and a profit could be shown.[46]

The problems, therefore, seemed to be passenger occupancy, intermediate travel between a train's origin and destination, the consequential under-utilization of space — and traffic marketing and promotion. The report's conclusions, while ignoring the political factors involved, laid responsibility for the passenger trains' deficits squarely with the railroads and declared that the "passenger train deficit is very real. . . but it can be wiped out!"

In this study, nothing has been uncovered that should prevent the railroads from earning a profit from their passenger services. Indeed, it appears inescapable that they would do so, if rail operations were as efficient as those of bus and airlines.

Rail expenses carry no handicap per unit produced. The rail passenger market has no growth barriers other than those artificially imposed. Successful operations and cost control are within the railroads' means, as are the keys to successful traffic promotion.

The present high cost of providing rail passenger

* A DC-6 could carry 60-72 passengers, versus a luxury rail coach which could carry between 56-64 passengers. By contrast, a modern DC-9 carries 101-141 passengers, while a modern Amtrak coach carries approximately 60 passengers.

services and the uncertain behavior of traffic volume are caused mainly by factors internal to the service and not by commercial competition nor by the private automobile.[47]

The report went on to say that "the operating deficit is not caused by low fares, by inadequate revenues or by high costs per car-mile," but by other causes, and listed eleven factors:

1. Short, heavy headend cars of insufficient cubic capacity;
2. Inadequate percentage loading of headend car space;
3. Revenue passenger cars with insufficient capacity;
4. Operation of an excessive percentage of empty seat-miles;
5. The burden of handling company equipment, materials and personnel;
6. Unnecessary losses from separate dining and lounge cars;
7. Excessive station and yard expenses;
8. High equipment-handling and servicing expense and inadequate daily car utilization;
9. Working rules, especially for train crews, that may be outmoded;
10. Failure to analyze existing cost data, or to keep records adequate for modern cost control and operations research;
11. Excessive state and local taxes.[48]

Its final conclusions stated that even "new trains" were not the sole remedy to the problem and that rail travel could be popular. "There is no other transportation operation in the country where the net result appears to be so susceptible to improvement."

There existed an unusual profit opportunity. "Nowhere else in railroading, or in all transportation, does such a profit opportunity exist."

Yet, more ominously, that "it is the majority opinion of the economic, financial and political experts consulted, that if the railroads cannot make passenger service pay, their days as privately-managed corporations are numbered." But, it remained hopeful. "If, on the other hand, new life is breathed into passenger train service, the national ëfeeling' about railroads will have come full circle again."[49]

In some ways, Young's efforts bore fruit and his campaign had its modest successes. The report lends credibility to Young's arguments (and confirms much of the findings of NYC's passenger research department in the process), but is less convincing about the answer to the question involving the human factor — could a train service be developed and provided that would be attractive enough to persuade the public to make greater use of it and less use of the automobile and airplane?

But, again, the public never saw the report.

What Young failed to recognize (and ignored by the RPI study) was the depth of the change that the railroad industry was facing in social and cultural life styles—changes in the market resulting from a metamorphosis away from the use of public transport services—and his failure to contemplate that the public support he courted and relied upon would fail to materialize. He had succeeded in stirring up public sentiment with the "hog ad" in 1946, but that support was short-lived. Like a super nova, it burnt itself out.

With the invention of the automobile and the popularity of the independence and convenience it offered, it was inevitable that government would eventually provide the means for the construction of roads for Americans to travel. The Transportation Act of 1916 would only be the first of a series of legislative bills authorizing the massive expenditure of public funds for transportation projects.

By 1946, when the Federal Airport Act was passed, the value of air transport had convincingly proven itself during the war so recently ended. Successive omnibus transportation legislation contained the allocation and authorization for funding of airport (and highway) development. These Acts would be passed at two-year intervals.

The basis for these bills was the country's defense. In an abrupt repudiation of the value and service of the railroad industry during the First and Second World Wars, the military began switching troop and equipment transport to highway and air. By the time of the Cold War, the military considered rail transport as obsolete and ineffectual as a transport option, and the railroads lost their biggest customer.

The passage of the Interstate Highway Act in 1956 placed the private rail carriers, still hobbled by the Transportation Act of 1920, at a considerable competitive disadvantage. Now the federal government was subsidizing highway transport on a much broader scale with no thought of the detrimental effects to the privately financed rail industry. The Act, in turn, invigorated an already well-established highway lobby made up of contractors, suppliers, truck and bus transporters, the automotive industry, oil companies, support services, etc., which became increasingly influential while rail transport's influence collapsed.

Labor practices were also under siege. Between 1952 and 1957 the "featherbedding" issue became headline news. With the advent of the diesel-electric locomotive, the demise of steam locomotion, and the introduction of Budd's revolutionary RDC, many seriously questioned the need to employ a fireman on a locomotive. NYC addressed the issue with the RDC as their "case in point."[50] But while the featherbedding issue raised legitimate concerns for the railroads, the confrontation also made the industry, on both sides of the argument, look foolish, inept, and inefficient in the eyes of the public.

Remember that 1956 also saw the introduction of Santa Fe's bi-level *El Capitan*. The new stainless steel cars from

Rock Island's *Aerotrain* (No. 3 - now in repose at the National Museum of Transportation in St. Louis, minus its diesel engine) is in commuter service at La Salle Street Station on August 19, 1964. Designed for short and medium haul service, that's how it was used by the Rock Island.

Budd were designed to increase passenger capacity and they were the antithesis of Young's theories.

The same period produced the "gallery" commuter coaches on the Midwestern commuter lines out of Chicago and in California on the Southern Pacific. Faced with the high costs of turning the many suburban trains at the end of each run, the contemporary "push-pull" concept (long used in Europe and adapted for use by NYC) was employed with a control cab being built into the rearend of the last coach. When the train reached its destination, the engineer merely walked to the other end to reverse the train's direction with the engine pushing the train instead of pulling it. The concept would become standard operating practice on other commuter lines and, later, on Amtrak's "corridor" runs.

The year 1956 saw the railroad industry's last (albeit abortive) effort to revive passenger service and deal with the passenger train dilemma, short of the traditional method—execution. By the end of 1957, with a stagnant economy, inflation, and a continuing decline in rail freight traffic, the only passenger train design that achieved a measure of popular success was the bi-level *El Capitan*—an all-coach *El Capitan*.

And when it became obvious that the lightweight experiments could not meet their objectives, the industry turned its attention and efforts to eliminating their passenger service altogether.

The failure of *Xplorer* and *Xplorer* has been blamed (and derided) in part because of their various mechanical weaknesses, which dampened their appeal. The industry's internal conflicts didn't help any, either. Ultimately, the projects were doomed by virtue of their inability to overcome America's desire to drive the automobile and its preoccupation with saving time traveling the airplane. Their failures, therefore, more properly should be blamed on the combination of factors which coincided in 1956 — a combination which any one organization, let alone one man, would have been powerless to overcome. The overwhelming sense of failure helped in their rapid and ignominious disappearance from the railroad scene.

With the death of Young in early 1958, the railroad industry lost one of its more creative and innovative leaders who, while controversial, had invariably focused attention on the industry's need to change with the times. The new trains concept didn't die with Young, however. While *Train X* (*Xplorer* on NYC and *Daniel Webster* on the New Haven) was quietly shunted into early retirement, and its Electro-Motive Division (EMD) counterpart, *Xplorer*, relegated to commuter service on the Rock Island, the Europeans continued pursuing the basic concept. Now, forty years after their demise, their lightweight descendants are plying the rails of Amtrak. It seems that Young's ideas were flawed by poor timing as well as by the limitations of inflexible public policies and management failures.

Some have argued that were it not for Young's campaign for a transcontinental passenger service, and in support of rail passenger travel in general, and of *Train X,* the passenger train would have met its demise ten years before it actually did - perhaps as early as 1958. Given a sympathetic government, perhaps Amtrak might have been created at the same time - at least NYC's researchers were recommending it. Others have argued that had the government and railroads done more, passenger service might have evolved into a form similar to that envisioned by Young. Both arguments are purely conjecture, of course, given the nature of the times and political climate.

Regardless, there is no doubt that Young played an important, perhaps a pivotal, role in sustaining the passenger train at a time when it sorely needed a champion; and focusing attention on its problems, causes and solutions. Indeed, one of the tragedies of his suicide was that while he had several disciples, when he was gone, there was no one to take his place. In Young the rail passenger could not have asked for a more articulate and talented defender; and his legacy goes well beyond the relics which today lay dormant in museums and which are portrayed in photographs as asterisks in the history of American transportation.

J. W. Swanberg

United Aircraft built its *Turbotrain* (designed by Alan Cripe) based on principles of *The Comet,* Robert Young, and Kenneth Browne. As Amtrak Turbo 52, the train is seen on Penn Central rails as Amtrak's *Yankee Clipper,* departing New Haven on August 2, 1975.

After dining in one of NYC's elegant dining rooms, such as this Budd creation (dining car No. 695), having a tray meal at one's seat lost much of its appeal.

Is Train X the Answer?

By Thomas J. Deegan, Jr.
President, the Federation for Railway Progress
Tracks, November 1951

Four years ago I had the good fortune to be present at a conference of American railway executives who were considering the possibilities of a new type passenger attain which, if adopted by our industry, might go a long way toward stemming the on-rushing tide of the passenger train deficit.

A few days ago, I had the fascinating experience of riding such a train in full revenue operation.

A twist to this story is that the rail trip did not take place in the most progressive country on the face of the earth, my home land—over the magnificent roadbed of one of our giant American rail systems, themselves shining examples of free enterprise.

On the contrary, the trip was made over the war-ravaged rails of the Spanish National Railroads on the *Talgo* train operating 400 miles, over the Pyrenees Mountains and through the starkly beautiful Spanish countryside from the French border south to the capital of Madrid.

The *Talgo* train is the product of Old World enterprise which frankly put me a little to shame as I witnessed its superb performance against odds such as we in American railroad circles seldom have to face politically, educationally or technologically.

Talgo, which was built in America by American Car & Foundry from specifications submitted by the Spaniards, is the most modern train in the world today, thoroughly revolutionary in design. It is low slung, articulated, lightweight and powered by an especially built 1150 hp diesel locomotive. Its on-time performance record for its first full year of operation is 99.56 per cent.

In Spain, the *Talgo* has replaced the bullfight as the chief topic of conversation. Over the rest of the Continent its fame has already spread far and wide. Almost no one entering Spain by rail from France fails to make a reservation on this remarkable train for the journey southbound. Frequently, tourists must wait over in San Sebastian until their names are reached on the waiting list.

Talgo is an all coach-all reserved seat, super deluxe passenger express. It goes from Irun to Madrid, a distance of 400 miles in eight and one half hours southbound and eight hours northbound, getting the benefit of the downgrade on the latter. Ordinary standard equipment trains make this run in fourteen hours.

I sat for more than an hour on the trip in the engine cab and watched us take curves at seventy miles an hour without the slightest lurching. Talgo's top possible speed is 120 miles an hour. With the exception of a small section of newly laid rails, the Spanish roadbed is just about as bad as one will find anywhere.

Yet, the ride was smooth and swift. The train consisted of a locomotive, one headend car which carried the air-conditioning machinery and the other mechanical gadgets for the whole train, and thirteen so-called trailer units, each seating sixteen persons. Three equipment cars were interspersed to handle the baggage and from which meals were served.

Dining is a delight. Meals are served at your place, airline style. Following the European custom, there is a fixed meal, no choices—with the entree is included wine-of-the-district, and brandy later.

Like the airlines, Talgo has its food put aboard at terminal points and operates only a hot plate in each of the three equipment cars. Luncheon is served southbound, dinner northbound. Unlike the airlines, Talgo charges prevailing rates for its meals.

In American dollars, the tariff for the one way trip between Irun and Madrid comes to about $10. *Talgo* engineers told me that not only was the original cost of the equipment about one third of the cost of equivalent number of seats in standard equipment, but the maintenance cost of both cars and rail were 75 per cent less.

The fact that this railroad progress came to pass in Old Spain is directly attributable to the Oriol family—one of the oldest and most respected in their country. The Oriols—father and son—who are financiers engaged in a variety of public interest projects, prompted the Talgo venture to bring railroad progress to Spain and to do it profitably at the same time. Obviously, *Talgo* can only reflect credit on the Franco Government, which the Oriols, as violent anti-Communists, ardently support. *Talgo* was built privately for the Oriols by ACF; it is operated over government-controlled facilities on a contract agreement. In the first year of revenue operation (Generalissimo Franco presided over its maiden run on July 14, 1950) *Talgo* has produced a modest operating profit.

The Oriols are hopeful that if this revenue-producing experiment proves out in Spain, the same principle can be expanded to cover passenger service throughout the entire European Continent.

It is here that we turn back to the conference of American railroad executives four years ago. The deficit were booming then, they are staggering now.

Ordinarily, any business that loses $508,500,000 a year is not considered a healthy enterprise. Last year the business of operating passenger train service in the United States according to ICC statistics issued in May, 1951, cost railroa investors that shocking sum.

Ordinarily, any business showing such a deficit would not be in existence a second year. The business of operating passenger train service (which, incidentally, includes the costly hauling of mail, baggage, and express) will continue for another year; in fact, it will have to continue for many another year as long as railroads are operated in the public interest.

It is obvious, therefore, that since the service cannot be abolished totally, the rail executives charged with this responsibility must apply more than ordinary ingenuity to the solution of this trying problem.

All intelligent segments of our industry, however, are alert to the situation and are actively seeking suitable remedies. One school of thought among such executives holds that after the unprofitable branch line and secondary main line trains have been removed, the remaining available service should be sold aggressively with some twentieth century advertising, merchandising, and promotional techniques to obtain maximum revenue. Collaterally, the original cost plus the cost of operating and maintaining the equipment necessary to do this job must be kept at a minimum by the application of modern technology.

One American railroad and one of the nation's leading car building companies have collaborated during the last two years to put onto American rails the counterpart, plus additional refinements, of the *Talgo*. This was the plan struck at the conference four years ago. Within the last three months one typical, experimental unit of such revolutionary equipment has had a successful test run.

The experiment has been designated as *Train X*. It weighs about one third as much per unit of floor space as standard equipment. It costs one third as much to construct.

Apart from cleaning, which is the largest item of car maintenance, mechanical repairs for *Train X* would cost only one third as much as mechanical repairs for conventional equipment.

The passenger deficit, according to the ICC formula, was $508,500,000 for 1950, a decrease of $141,100,000 from the all-time peak deficit of $649,600,000 in 1949. However, adjusting for mail pay received in 1950 but earned in previous years, the realistic 1950 passenger deficit would be $615,000,000.

Using the official ICC figure of $508,500,000, the passenger deficit absorbed 32.9 per cent of the 1950 freight new railway operating income.

Hopefully, *Train X* is the answer. It is working in Spain.

TLC Collection

Preliminary drawings of *Xplorer* from P-S showed a futuristic train traversing a tight curve with an identical train passing in the opposite direction.

a preview of Pullman-Standard's

train X

the new train the nation's leading carbuilder is building

for increased speed—safety —pleasure for passengers, lower initial operating and maintenance costs for railroads.

featuring
- low center of gravity
- roll compensating design
- bidirectional air-glide ride

What Train X is Like...

What Makes It Different?

The first *Train X* has been delivered to the New York Central by its builder, Pullman-Standard. A similar train is on order for the New Haven. The locomotive for the NYC train, assembled by Baldwin-Lima-Hamilton, is the subject of a separate article in this issue.

The NYC *Train X*, which that road will call the *Xplorer*, will have its aluminum exterior painted in blue and yellow. The NH version will introduce an innovation—an exterior surface of colored aluminum. Each NH car has a dark gray finish contrasted with natural metallic aluminum.

The surface of the colored aluminum will be highly abrasion resistant. The coating is a layer of crystal clear aluminum oxide built up electrochemically as part of the metal. It is practically as hard as sapphire, which is basically aluminum oxide.

The train consists of 9 45-1/2 foot units. The entire body structure of each unit weighs less than 7,000 lb, including the end sections. This is about 150 lb per lineal feet, or 40 per cent of the weight of a conventional car body. Interior trim and equipment bring the weight to 13,000 lb for the 48-passenger compartment, or 300 lb per foot of length. Equipment in the end lockers, wheel wells, the couplers, etc., add another 10,000 lb. Wheels, axles and suspension details bring the total weight to 28,500 lb per unit. The entire 9-section train weighs less than 135 tons empty (excluding the locomotive, which weighs 68 tons) and about 165 tons loaded—about 675 lb per seat.

In the "box in a box" construction, the inside finish "floats" on the structure through flexible supports at all points of contact. The floor is mounted to the stringers on rubber pads especially designed for vibration mounting. Similarly, the interior side and end elements are attached to the structure by vibration mounts or rubber strips specially designed for flexible mounting.

Metal panels are either treated with a sprayed or damping material or they are damped by the plastic material used for the inside finish. Double-wall sound barriers are used at the wheel wells.

The floor floats on resilient pads which correct for vibration in three planes—longitudinal, vertical and lateral. No adhesive or bolting is required between the pad and the flooring or between the pad and the underframe. The pads are neoprene and resistant to oil, grease and permanent set.

Foamed-in-place insulation is used in the belly of the car, reportedly the first time material of this nature has been used in a railway passenger car. The initial reason for using insulation of this type was for its thermal value. Of nearly equal significance, however, is its ability to keep sound transmission at a low level. This insulation also has the advantage of filling in all right angles and nooks and crevices. It also acts as a sheet stiffener.

An extra wide air space between inner and outer panes in the window (1 in. in contrast to the usual 1/4 in.) decreases "acoustic coupling" and is particularly effective in the speech frequency band, or the range of noise that interferes with conversation. This wider spacing transmits a minimum of vibration (hence noise) from the outer to the inner window.

Air duct noise has also been studied to keep it to a minimum. The recirculating duct has a special acoustical lining in the bottom. The main air duct has waved sheets inside for 4 feet between the air conditioning unit and the beginning of the duct proper. This gives the air a sinusoidal path for this length. The duct itself has top and sides of 1-in. glass fiber insulation covered with a heavy vinyl plastic coating on the inside surface.

Passenger-Proof Interior

Primary objective of the interior car design was to make it attractive while requiring the least possible maintenance without compromising weight or cost factors. None of the materials used in the car interior requires paint and all are easy to clean.

The curved section of the ceiling is glass fiber insulation 1-in. thick, formed to the contour with vinyl facing prebonded to it. This gives a finished ceiling plus insulation at the same time. The vinyl covering can be washed and does not need painting. Each sheet extends from the center duct to the side and is 6-1/2 feet long.

The walls are faced with either a vinyl material or a Melamine (a hard plastic like Formica or Micarta). The two types of plastic are mixed to give different decorative effects. Both types are bonded in place by .040-in. aluminum backing forming the inside sheets. Insulation goes behind these sheets as a conventional cars.

There are three basic color schemes and end wall decorations. End finish materials are various decorative patterns using vinyls and hard plastics. Flooring of 1/16-in. vinyl tile in 9 in. squares with different color patterns gives distinctive floor treatment.

Seats are specially designed for light weight with comfort and ease of cleaning. Cushioning is of foam plastic (similar to foam rubber). The base of the seat fits flush with the floor all around. There are no dirt pockets in the base or between the base and the floor. The base of one seat also serves as the foot rest for the seat behind.

Upholstery is essentially of animal fiber for the seat and back sections where the passengers' body weight rests, while vinyl trim is used on the head rolls, the arm rests and the forward part of the seat cushion. Backs of the seats are also of vinyl to withstand scuffing. Again for comfort, the head rolls are exceptionally soft.

The upholstery is removable for cleaning by action of a zipper in the facing edges of adjoining seats. The seats are contoured, and have ash trays in each arm under the lever for reclining the seat.

The need for shades, blinds and draperies is eliminated by tinted window glass. The degree of tint is graduated with the lightest area in the approximate horizontal center. Large (26 in. by 66 in.) windows are used throughout the train.

How Air Springs Work

Air, rather than coil or leaf springs, are used in *Train X* for two principal reasons—to give constant height and constant frequency. It was thought that weight changes, which go as high as 40 per cent on some axles, would affect the stiffness and frequency of a coil spring too much for satisfactory riding comfort.

With the articulated arrangement if coil springs with their straight line characteristic or leaf springs with a nearly straight line characteristic were to be used, some axles would have to be designated specifically for operation at the end of the train only and others for operation within the train with an adjacent car hung on them. The air spring keeps the body height constant whether an axle end is supporting only its own body weight, as at the end of the train, or whether the non-axle end of the adjoining pair of units is hung from it.

The air springs in *Train X* are similar to those in use on buses. The rubber changes in diameter but slightly and this

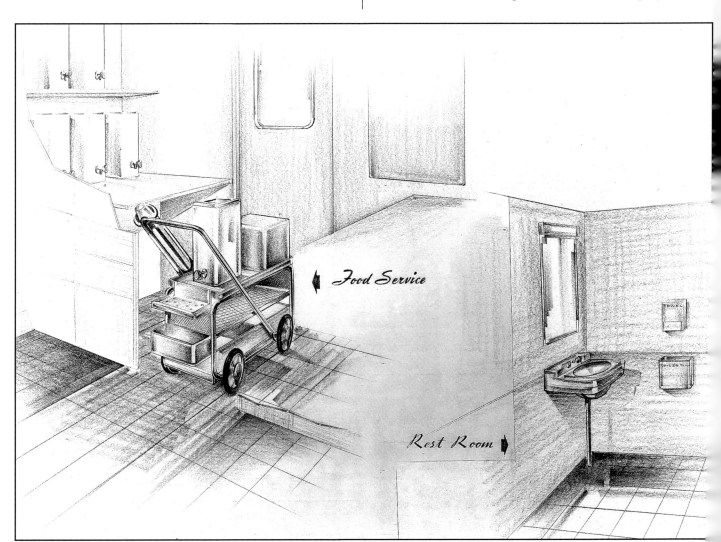

TLC Collectio

Artist's rendering of the "Cruisin' Susan" food service dolly, and a rendition of the rest facilities to be provided lent a vie of the train's amenities.

A nearly identical rendering was made for the New Haven only with a city background.

is due mainly to the deflection—not to stretching. Stretching is largely prevented by steel rings.

Constant height is maintained by adjusting the pressure in the air spring. It is set at full on a car in the middle of the train supporting the end of an adjacent unit. The pressure is set at 60 per cent when the car is at the end of the train to compensate for the lesser weight on the springs.

Train X introduces an aluminum alloy new to underframe construction. This corrosion-resistant high strength aluminum alloy (Specification 6061) has been for many years in other fields in its fully heat-treated temper (+T6). It has been used in its partial heat treatment (T4) in railway cars, but this is the first such T6 application.

The underframe is entirely fabricated from the 6061-T6 alloy (permitting weight savings over and above those attained with the 6061-T4 alloy) with the exception of the center end sill and the center sill extension on each end. The wheel wells and end sills are framed with welded high-tensile, low alloy steel. The center sill will resist a compressive force of 300,000 lb.

The entire superstructure is like-wise fabricated from aluminum sheet and extrusions. This superstructure, while tubular in shape, is basically of conventional structural design. The side posts and carlines are structural shapes formed from aluminum sheets while most other members are extruded aluminum shapes.

The outer skin is also of aluminum as are the two crash posts on each end, each of which can withstand a 300,000 lb collision force. The outside skin is Alclad aluminum (i.e., covered with pure aluminum coating). A non-metallic separator coating between aluminum and steel sections, as well as between adjoining aluminum sections, prevents accumulation of moisture—undesirable because of its accelerating effect on corrosion and electrolytic action.

Auxiliary electrical loads are all carried by a head-end power unit in the locomotive which furnishes 480-volt, 3-phase 60-cycle power. Total load for the 9-unit train is 283.5 kw, including the maximum air conditioning load of 144 kw.

A 400-hp diesel engine on the locomotive supplies the auxiliary power for the train. It is distributed through the cars by aluminum bus bars above the ceiling. Connection

TLC Collection

P-S offered three variations for the car interior designs. All were similar.

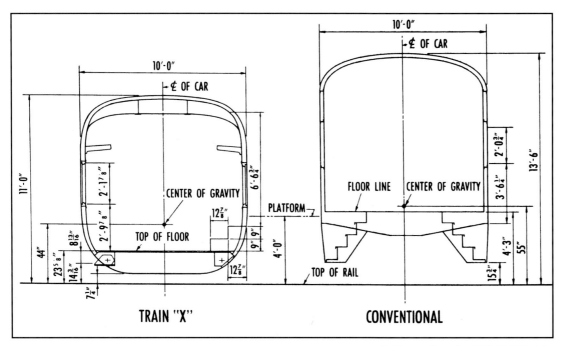

Pullman–Standard/TLC Collection

This is how the Train X compared with the cross section of a conventional coach.

between the cars is over the vestibules and is automatic upon coupling.

Each car has a completely self-contained air conditioning unit which plugs into the train line. Distribution of the cooled air is through the same duct as the heating air. It also contains the fluorescent lighting. As in heating, the air distributed is 40 per cent fresh and 60 per cent recirculated air. Discharge of the air into the car is through two strips of adjustable slot diffusers, one on each side of the air duct. The air conditioning unit is entirely self-contained and factory sealed.

The water system uses electric jackets for instantaneous heating of the water. Water can be added from either side and it is stored in a stainless tank above the washroom ceilings in each of the vestibule cars. Water flow is by gravity from this tank rather than by pressure. The non-vestibule cars do not have wash, toilet or drinking water facilities.

Unconventional Brake System

One large and one small air line extend through the train. The large line is termed the supervisory line, the other the straight air line.

For a service brake application the engineman moves the control lever for as much brake as he wants. The further he moves the brake handle the heavier the application. Thus the *Train X* brake application depends on how far the lever is moved rather than on how long it remains in the application position as on regular equipment.

Moving the control lever sets up an electric circuit which energizes magnet valves on each car, causing air from the reservoirs to flow into the brake cylinders and the straight air line reaches the amount set on the control lever, further air flow stops (except to make up for any leakage) and the brakes remain applied at the pressure set by the engineman.

The second, or supervisory line, supplies air to the car reservoirs continuously, whether the brake is on or off. It also controls emergency application. Any depletion of supervisory line pressure causes maximum brake cylinder pressure, whether the depletion occurs from an outside cause, as a break-in-two, or by the engine man's action in moving his control lever to its extreme position.

Failure of the electric control circuit automatically causes the straight air line to take over the brake application pneumatically. If movement of the control lever fails to build up straight air-line pressure, a pressure differential is created in the control arrangement.

This differential puts air in the straight line and

Both: *TLC Collection*

Two variations of the interior design that P-S offered for the *Train X*.

applies the brakes on each car in the same manner as the magnet valves but somewhat delayed, due to (1) a short period of time to build up the pressure differential, and (2) the pneumatic delay in filling the line from the front to the rear of the train (although the delay generally would not be enough for the engineman to notice).

The system has another feature, intended to permit a car to be used anywhere in the train without underbraking under one condition and overbraking under another. When a vestibule car is used at the end of the train, where it is not supporting an adjoining car on its end, the braking force on its axle is reduced to 60% to conform to the lesser weight on the axle.

When a vestibule car supports an adjoining car on its end, 100% braking force is applied. The switchover is made by changing the air flow circuit between two diaphragms—one of which balances brake cylinder pressure against 60% of the straight air line pressure, the other against full line pressure.

While this system, known as the LWE, cannot be used to control cars with standard automatic brake equipment, the locomotive can be equipped with a triple valve device that will allow the towing locomotive to actuate the pneumatic straight air feature and to charge the reservoirs.

The cars are equipped with the new "Cobra" shoe tread brake. One shoe is used per wheel, and it is mounted on top rather than acting on the side of the wheel as is typical of other single-shoe brakes. Each shoe is applied by its own cylinder.

All Electric Heating

Train X is heated exclusively by electricity. With 40% makeup fresh air (vs. the usual 25% fresh air) about 30% of the heat comes from the electric strip heaters in the sides below the windows (from which it discharges into the car by convection through slots under the windows). The remaining 70% of the heat is from the overhead duct. Controls give either one-third or full heat. When car temperature drops below the control setting, one-third of the heat capacity is applied in both the floor and overhead heat by connecting the elements of Y. If this first step cannot heat the car to the desired setting, a second contact switches the heaters to delta connection giving full heat output from the same set of units.

For standby heating the floor heat only is used to avoid the additional loss by introducing fresh air.

Batteries in the locomotive are used to crank the engine and to operate the control circuits for the brake circuit (64 volts). One small 60-volt battery in each car will operate emergency lights up to 5 hours. These emergency lights are strictly minimum, comprising two small bulbs in each passenger compartment and one in each vestibule. They are not intended for full car lighting under emergency conditions.

Lighting in the NYC train is by four rows of fluorescent tubes in the overhead heating duct and one along either side for indirect lighting. Illumination is both directly downward and out the sides. The New Haven train will have the two outside rows for indirect lighting and individual reading lights mounted on the baggage rack over each seat.

How the "Air Spring" Operates

This outline sketch shows the main elements of the *Train X* air spring. The air within the spring has an open path at all times to the tank above, which increases the volume of air on which the spring effectively operates for cushioning without increasing the size of the rubber bellows itself.

Leveling and constant car body height is achieved by admitting air from the supervisory line or discharging air from the tank to the atmosphere. A slide valve is connected to the tank which allows movement 1/4 inch either way from the center without putting air in or out of the tank.

If the tank is depressed more than this amount air will flow from the supervisory air line into it to increase the pressure in the tank and the bellows to raise the level to the predetermined height. If the train load should lighten the

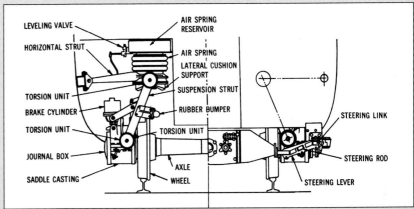

tank will rise and the slide valve will open another port which will discharge air from the tank to the atmosphere and return the car to the proper level. Road shocks which cause the car to bounce up and down will of course admit or discharge minor quantities of air but this is said to create no problem.

Air spring pressure on a car within the train (and therefore supporting an adjacent car end) are 90 psi with a full passenger load, 70 psi empty. For the axle at the end of the train these pressures are 56 and 45 psi.

—*Railway Age*

Diesel Mec-Hydro Powers Xplorer

New concepts in design and arrangement have been applied to the *Xplorer* locomotive just as they have to the train it hauls. This 174,000-lb passenger power unit delivers all of its 1,000 traction horsepower through a two-axle front truck.

This front truck is a complete power package having the diesel engine, hydraulic transmission, drive shafts and axle drives all mounted on it. The locomotive is suspended from both trucks by body swing links designed to allow the locomotive to operate through curves at high speeds. The complete power truck is arranged so that it can be removed and replaced quickly to obtain maximum locomotive utilization.

The 1,000-hp propulsion diesel is a German-built, high-speed, V-type engine which delivers its power through a Mec-hydro hydraulic transmission. This torque converter-mechanical drive is also German-made. While both are new to American high speed service, the Maybach diesel has been used for over 15 years on European railroads, and this type of transmission has won acceptance.

The transmission has four speeds in forward and in reverse which are claimed to give high efficiency over the entire speed range. From the continuous tractive force of 21,000 lbs at 12.6 mph, full horsepower output is maintained up to the maximum speed of 120 mph.

Mounted in the body of the locomotive is an eight-cylinder Maybach engine driving a 300-kw, 440-volt, 3-phase, 60-cycle generator. This engine has many components interchangeable with those in the propulsion engine. The generator supplies electric power for the entire train.

While the length and width of this 0-4-4-0 passenger unit are not unusual, the overall height has been held to only 11 ft to match the contour of the lightweight Train X cars it hauls.

Maybach Engine

The engine's appearance is not unlike that of more conventional V-type diesels. Apparent differences are the vertical shaft turbocharger mounted between the two cylinder banks on the top of the engine, the turbocharger intercoolers, and the short overall length of the engine itself. In Europe this power plant is known as the "tunnel" engine. This comes from the shape of the crankcase which combines the frame and bedplate into one piece, and from the large main bearing bores. Roller type main bearings are used instead of conventional friction bearings.

Normal operating speed of the propulsion engine is 1,550 rpm. It has 12 cylinders with cylinder bore of 7.8 in.

and stroke of 7.9 in. All combustion air is cooled after leaving the turbocharger and before it goes into the cylinders. The engine has a weight of approximately 10 lb per hp—less than that of U.S. locomotive diesels.

Both the propulsion engine and the smaller auxiliary engine operate on a four-stroke cycle. The smaller engine is very similar to the traction engine except that it has only eight cylinders. Operating at 1,200 rpm, it has a rating of 570 hp.

The crankshaft has solid disc webs used also as the inner races for the roller main bearings. This shaft design permits use of longer crankpins and closer cylinder spacing. The short disc-webbed crankshaft with large diameter crankpins is claimed to reduce crankshaft twist and torsional vibration.

The connecting rods are fork-and-blade type. Pistons are of two-piece construction with removable forged steel crowns which carry the three compression rings. The water-cooled cast iron liners are supported at the top, center and bottom to insure exact alignment and for maximum reinforcement. Dual seals are used at the bottom to insure exact alignment and for maximum reinforcement. Dual seals are used at the bottom of the liner with a tell-tale hole in the block which drains the space between the two seals. This is to detect leaks and to prevent water dilution.

Each cylinder head has three inlet and three exhaust valves. The heat load per valve is low, and because these valves are arranged in a circle around the combustion chamber, gas flow is improved and the rigidity of the head is increased.

There is a spherical combustion chamber in the center of the head into which the nozzle of the unit-type injector delivers fuel through a single relatively large hole. The injectors are controlled by a worm drive connected to the governor control mechanism. Over each cylinder bank are two camshafts, one for the exhaust and the other for the intake valves. The low-inertia valve rockers have hydraulic lash adjusters.

This engine has three separate lubricating oil systems—piston cooling, valve gear, and major running parts (crankshaft and connecting rod bearings). There is also a prestart lubricating system which insures lubrication before the engine is running. The governor is of variable speed hydraulic relay type driven by gears and incorporating a low oil pressure shutdown.

Mec-hydro Transmission

The Baldwin Maybach hydraulic transmission is fully automatic—responding to both locomotive speed and engine load demands. It consists of a permanently filled hydraulic torque converter, and a four-speed mechanical gear box with three pairs of helical gears operating in conjunction with positive over-running claw clutches. Operating controls are an integral part of the transmission.

The disengaging torque converter has an impeller driven by the engine, and a turbine with two sets of blading which shift along its axis to engage or disengage the output shaft. Shifting of the turbine rotor imposes a reverse set of blading in the oil stream to give a weak backward torque so that the claw clutches will engage smoothly. The control system does the shifting automatically, and is arranged to prevent reversing of the transmission before the locomotive comes to a complete stop, even though the operator throws the reverser.

The converter is permanently filled with oil making the locomotive quickly responsive to any throttle position. Gears are always meshed, and the changes are accomplished by engaging or disengaging the claw clutches. The transmission is cooled by water bypassed from the radiator system through the water jacket surrounding the torque converter and the transmission oil heat exchanger.

Axle Drive

The axle drive housings are heavy cast steel to protect against external damage and to give maximum support for the gears. The spiral bevel gears and pinions are lubricated with a forced feed system from an integral gear type pump which also supplies oil to all the drive unit bearings. There are no waste-packed lubricators.

Torque reaction is absorbed by a member supported on the truck frame by a heavy-duty rubber-cushioned snubber. Drive shafts between the engine, transmission, and axle drives are equipped with flanged connections for easy removal. The universal joints all have sealed roller bearings. Timken roller bearings are used in the transmission and on the axle journals.

Automatic Control

The cab is conventionally arranged and this unit is equipped with GRS automatic train control for operation on the NYC. The diesel engine is in a compartment extending up through the locomotive body and is inspected from inside the locomotive only by opening a series of doors around and over the power plant.

Because of the relative movement between the truck-mounted diesel and the body, flexible connections have to be provided in the fuel and cooling water lines. Radiators for the power plants and for the transmission are at the rear of the locomotive body. The coupler at the front is a conventional retractable E type which makes it possible to handle this unit with a standard locomotive. At the rear is the special coupler required for the *Xplorer* equipment.

T.W. Dixon, Jr. Collection

NYC 20 contained a 1000 HP Maybach V-12 diesel engine which was connected to a hydraulic transmission called "Mechydro," with four speed ranges. It tended to overheat in its high-speed mode and spent much of its life in the shops. A smaller 570 HP Maybach V-8 auxiliary diesel powered a generator for lights, heat, and air conditioning. Baldwin imported the diesels and special-ordered many of the components from other manufacturers. Designated RP-210 by Baldwin, this and the two New Haven units were among the last Baldwin locomotives built. Note the wind deflectors and mirror added by NYC.

Shortly after Alleghany took control of the New York Central, Young and his delegates on the Board of Directors caused the company to create two "traffic" research groups, one each in the freight and passenger departments. The passenger research group was charged with investigating methods whereby the company's escalating passenger service deficits might be reduced and its passenger services reshaped into a self-supporting, and eventually profitable operation. The freight group was asked to seek new sources of traffic and means of improving the net revenue* yields of existing and possible future freight traffic.

After initial research and analysis of the company's "passenger services" (as defined by the Interstate Commerce Commission) for 1955 and 1956, the Passenger Research Bureau made several preliminary observations based upon traffic studies, cost and revenue information generated by NYC's new computer accounting system just coming into service. NYC was also one of the sponsors of the University of Michigan's first annual national travel market surveys which generated the market information used in the studies.

1. New York Central's "passenger services" actually consisted of three very different types of operation: the inner-city transport of people, the transport of commuters within urban areas, and the inter-city transport of mail, parcels and newspapers.
2. Preliminary studies indicated trains primarily operated for the inter-city transport of people generated revenues in excess of their direct operating costs; the other two types of service were not meeting their direct costs.
3. The company's whole package of inter-city passenger services was out-dated and no longer responsive to the needs of the market. The most favorable market for rail passenger service was for trips of between 100 to 500 miles in length, generally involving a total trip time of less than 12 hours.
4. The practice of combining "head-end" traffic with the inter-city carriage of passengers on a single train resulted in a high cost service which could not meet the needs of either market.
5. The scheduling plans and operating methods used for all-passenger passenger services were wasteful and unnecessarily expensive in their use of equipment, manpower and facilities.
6. Most of the company's principal passenger service terminals and larger stations were designed and built around the turn of the century anticipating continued traffic increases that never materialized. This resulted in facility costs far in excess of those required for present and foreseeable future traffic.
7. Most passenger stations were poorly situated in terms of their accessibility to each community's principal sources of traffic.

After further studies the Bureau developed specific suggestions for major changes and improvements in the company's passenger service policies and operating practices:

A. Passenger service operations as defined by the ICC be

H.H. Harwood, Jr.

Following the demise of NYC's travel tailored schedules in 1958, mail and express trains were combined with intercity passenger trains on lengthened schedules. One such train was No. 90, the *Chicagoan,* shown leaving Cleveland with a lot of head end traffic behind its three Es in the spring of 1960. In the background is a Nickel Plate freight with piggybacks led by a GP-9 and two RS-2s. Tracks are (L-R) rapid transit tracks, NKP main, CUT main, NYC freight line.

*Defined as the revenue remaining after direct expenses are paid

divided into three separately managed and operated entities: inter-city passenger, commuter, and inter-city mail & parcel.

B. Intercity passenger (i.e., "people") services be re-designed to be more in keeping with changing market needs while simultaneously making them substantially less costly to operate.

C. Present equipment for "people" traffic be replaced with new equipment incorporating these principal features:

Improved comfort and convenience for passengers
Capable of intensive use
Simplicity and ease of maintenance and cleaning
Lower operating costs; i.e. more effective use of man-power, lower traction horsepower and reserve fleet requirements, reduced fuel consumption, etc.

D. Consideration be given to combining NYC's inter-city passenger services with those of the B&O in an inde-pendently financed, managed and operated entity. (Later expanded to include the Pennsylvania.)

E. Commutation services be discontinued unless the communities served agree to supply sufficient financial support for them to be self-sustaining. (It was recog-nized this could lead to serious problems in the New York and Boston metropolitan areas, where it was sug-gested they be combined with those of the New Haven in new completely independent entities with the intent of enabling the use of lower cost operating facilities, equipment and systems while making their financial distress more transparent, thereby simplifying efforts to obtain public financial support and/or per-mission to rationalize, reduce or eliminate the ser-vices.)

F. The mail & parcel service be reshaped into an expe-dited, scheduled freight service eliminating all loading and unloading activities by railway personnel. (This reflected the fact that the post office had just discon-tinued most of its R.P.O. and first class railway mail ser-vices, and that parcel (express) traffic was rapidly leav-ing rail in favor of the lower cost, improved service, and wider territorial coverage offered by highway competitors.)

G. Principal passenger stations be studied with the intent of improving their accessibility to/from principal markets, reducing all associated costs, gaining municipal participa-tion in their maintenance and for insuring the availabili-ty of local transit services. (It was recognized this might involve winning public support and participation in building a new station in a more suitable location.)

The Bureau was then requested to incorporate these findings and suggestions in a reshaping of the company's prin-cipal intercity passenger services in a way that would be sub-stantially less costly to operate and would reverse the con-tinuing erosion of traffic and revenues. The result was a "Travel Tailored Schedule Plan" introduced in the October 1956 Fall Timetable. The primary focus of the plan was on daytime (i.e. coach) travel for trips of 500 miles or less, with longer trips, overnight and sleeper travel given a second pri-ority.

The company's traditional policy of operating its passen-ger trains in fleets was discarded in favor of fast "passen-ger-only" trains operated at convenient hours between all larger markets. With the exception of a limited number of long distance trains, the schedule was based on the use of small trains (i.e. 5 to 7 cars with a single fleet of cars and locomotives), with more intensive use of a substantially smaller fleet of cars and locomotives. A pilot project was also suggested for relocating the Albany station west of downtown, near the new government center.

Meanwhile, NYC's system superintendent of operations, Charles Clark, a devotee of Perlman, "discovered" what was being planned and "raised the roof." The new schedules would wreak havoc with freight train operations.

Two new trains, Nos. 73 and 74, which operated between Albany and Buffalo, were designed to operate with five to seven cars, i.e. four to six coaches and a cafe-lounge. These cars would be pulled by a single passenger engine. He ordered a change in their consist, adding five to seven bag-gage cars, and randomly "repositioned" dead-head coaches and sleepers thus creating fourteen to seventeen car trains which necessitated the addition of a second or third diesel unit with a corresponding less-than-optimal schedule perfor-mance. He then called Perlman's attention to this "ridiculous, wasteful operation" and there ensued a major internal crisis, followed by instructions to eliminate trains Nos. 73 and 74 - and to stop all planning for the next stage of the travel tai-lored schedules.

In July 1957, before the new schedule had time to take root, the new schedule plan was abruptly canceled by exec-utive order of the president and most of the new, fast "pas-senger-only" schedules were converted to slow, multi-stop "head-end traffic" trains with coaches at one end. The New York Public Utilities Commission, having approved the origi-nal "Travel Tailored Schedules," refused to accept this revision and ordered the New York State portions of the original plan restored. (These restored portions remained in effect until Amtrak took over in 1971, and are still operating today.)

Later, NYC's management announced its intention of abandoning its passenger business altogether. The Passenger Research Bureau and most of the Passenger Department were disbanded and concerted efforts initiated to remove all remaining passenger services.

Sources:

J. S. Gallagher, Jr., Passenger Research Bureau documents,
Documents prepared by NYC legal department staff
August 1996

Meanwhile... Over at Budd

While P-S and ACF were building experimental lightweight trains in 1956, Budd was building experimental trains/cars of its own. Hoping to catch a portion of the market which was then in its infancy, two of Budd's designs were to meet most of the criteria of the lightweight aspirations: the *Keystone* cars (sometimes referred to as "tubular"), built for the Pennsylvania Railroad; and the Pioneer III prototype car.

The *Keystone* cars were a lightweight and simplified variation of conventional stainless steel coaches, but intended to be pulled by a conventional or newly designed (Aerotrain?) locomotive. Power for the electrical systems was provided from a diesel generator which was located in the first car.

The interiors would be simple and Spartan—made of plastics and stainless steel. Each car consisted of a coach section, a principal feature of which was that it would be located in the drop center of the car's main body, with a smoking lounge on the platform over the trucks at each end of the car. They would be heated by electric convection with air conditioning provided through a self-contained system in each car.

The Pennsylvania Railroad was the only buyer for the *Keystone* lightweight experiment. It proved to be unstable in service and consequently spent much of its life in storage after experiencing a brief period of service between New York City and Washington.

The Pioneer III was another design which was a refinement of Budd's earlier stainless steel designed coaches. The car was 85 feet in length; stood 11 feet, 9 inches high; had a light weight of 83,000 pounds, and a center of gravity of 43-1/2 inches versus conventional cars which had a center of gravity of 52 inches. It seated 88 persons and was meant to combine the attributes of other experimental lightweight equipment. The power to operate its electrically dependent systems (i.e. heat and air conditioning) would come from headend power, or from the then standard steam lines and battery power.

Its interiors would be low-cost, made of plastics, and simplified to reduce construction and maintenance costs. The car's exterior design was rounded, like the tubular design of the Keystone, and would eventually serve as a starting point for Budd's later attempts at newer and improved passenger equipment (Metroliner, commuter coaches, Amfleet equipment, etc.).

George Melvin

The *Roger Williams*, the Budd-built "train of the future" is seen leaving Boston's South Station circa 1964 as a three-car train when it was pressed into commuter service.

Meanwhile, Budd was also working on commuter double-decker, or "gallery" cars, conventional dome cars, Santa Fe's "high-level" or double-decker passenger cars for the *El Capitan,* a modified RDC train (eventually bought by the New Haven), and its "Siesta coach," which came to be known as "slumbercoach" ("sleepercoach" on NYC).

All of these cars were to debut in 1956—and with the exception of Budd's more traditional lightweight equipment designs, they would share a similar fate by being quickly forgotten.

TLC Collection

John S. Gallagher, Jr.

The past meets what was expected to be the future. The *Aerotrain* passes an interlocking tower.

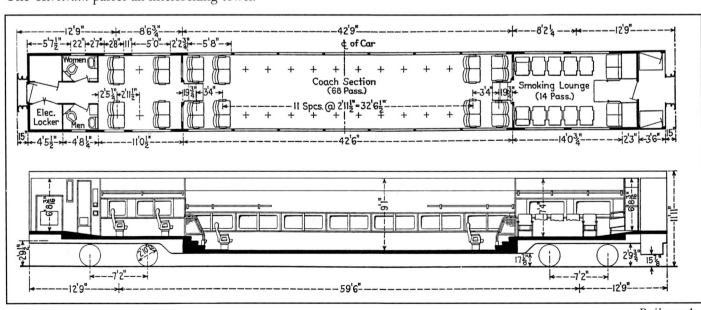

Railway Age

The plan for the Pennsylvania *Keystone* cars.

J. R. Quinn Collection

The Pennsylvania's *Keystone* cars are seen in this 1956 scene being pulled by one of the Pennsylvania's classic E-8 locomotives near Lewiston, Pennsylvania. The "tubular" design, like its experimental counterparts, did not catch on and suffered a similar fate.

TLC Collection

Budd's entry into the experimental "trains of the future" was a variation on its popular RDC design. With control cabs located on either end of the six-car train, called the *Roger Williams*, it fulfilled the requirements of the New Haven - but only the New Haven - which bought the only set built. The four RDC coaches in the middle were without controls, unlike the standard RDC units. Parts of the *Roger Williams* survived into the Amtrak era.

The New Haven Railroad's *Comet* was the genesis for the trains of the future, designed to be economical in mechanical operation as well as in labor productivity.

NYC Has New Passenger Service Idea

The New York Central's new fall schedules, to become effective October 28, "are based on more than 24 months of market research into what the traveler wants," Ernest C. Nickerson, vice-president—passenger sales and service, said when announcing the new timetables.

Mr. Nickerson, discussing what he called the NYC's "new passenger service concept," said it is based on a four-point program, of which the new fall schedules, Mr. Nickerson added, "will offer a better selection of fast trains at popular departure times with convenient arrivals." Running times of many existing trains have been speeded up through elimination of seldom-used stops, and several fast new trains have been added. Departures have been arranged generally so that patrons are offered the choice of early morning, noon, early evening and night trains between major points.

The other three phases of the new passenger service concept—which will be introduced on the railroad as development warrants—include a long-range program of redesigning passenger equipment to meet the comfort and convenience requirements for short, medium and long-distance travel. The NYC also is studying new methods and procedures to make it easier to buy tickets, make reservations and obtain information.

Lastly, the road's long-range program to develop and service its passenger business will be backed by an aggressive merchandising campaign using the latest techniques of research, marketing and sales.

The entire program is based upon the results of the vast market research project, which was undertaken to determine on the Central's system the quantity of travel, type of travel preferred, flow patterns, and departure and arrival time preferences.

Where previously each passenger train has attempted to serve some seven purposes—such as handling mail, express, baggage, operating needs, and short, medium and long-distance passengers—under the new schedules the primary concern will be the convenience to passengers. In many instances, separate trains will be operated to accommodate mail, express and baggage.

These two photos show the *Aerotrain* departing Englewood for Chicago on a beautiful summer's mid-day on July 29, 1956. Once in daily operation it failed to impress its passengers with its rough ride.

The *Aerotrain* slows to a stop at Englewood on July 29, 1956. It would call at Englewood for years to come, but for its eventual owner - Rock Island.

RAILWAY AGE

One of Five Simmons-Boardman Railway Publications

World Premiere

of a new concept in passenger-train travel—in Chicago, August 31st!

The new General Motors experimental passenger train will make its debut at the General Motors "Powerama"* in Chicago August 31st to September 25th. This ten-coach, high-speed, lightweight train suggests radical new concepts in integrated design of motive power and cars to increase attractiveness of service and make possible great reductions in first cost, operation and upkeep of passenger transportation equipment.

*Powerama—An exposition at Soldier Field to acquaint the public with what General Motors is doing in the general powering field.

ELECTRO-MOTIVE DIVISION
GENERAL MOTORS
La Grange, Illinois • Home of the Diesel Locomotive
In Canada: GENERAL MOTORS DIESEL, LTD., London, Ontario

GENERAL MOTORS LOCO MOTIVE

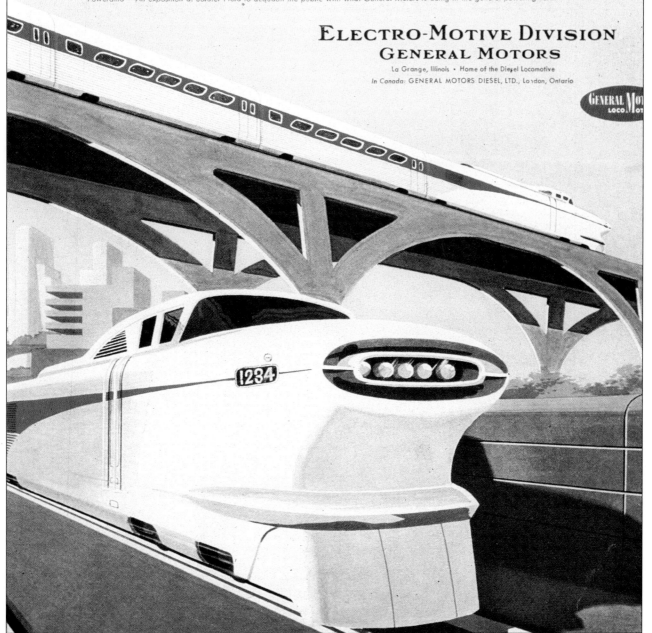

The *Aerotrain* passes the Samuel Insull Chicago, South Shore and South Bend Railroad near the latter's eastern-most terminus in August 1956.

The *Ohio Xplorer's* appearance on the railroad scene created a stir in railroad circles, but the average traveler was fascinated with the ease and convenience of the automobile, such as the Oldsmobile at right, waiting patiently for the *Xplorer* to clear the crossing.

This view of *Xplorer's* rearmost coach, shows in fine detail the coupler arrangement. In this view, the socket which receives the patented coupler from the trailing coach is concealed behind the white plate. The AAR coupler is removable; in this view it is mounted for use in turning the train in Cleveland and Cincinnati. The photo was taken at Galion, Ohio in October 1956.

When the *Xplorer* ran it was a good looking train. Looks aren't everything, however, and like a book, its exterior belied its contents.

The cast emblems on the sides of the Xplorer added a touch of class to the unusual looking locomotive.

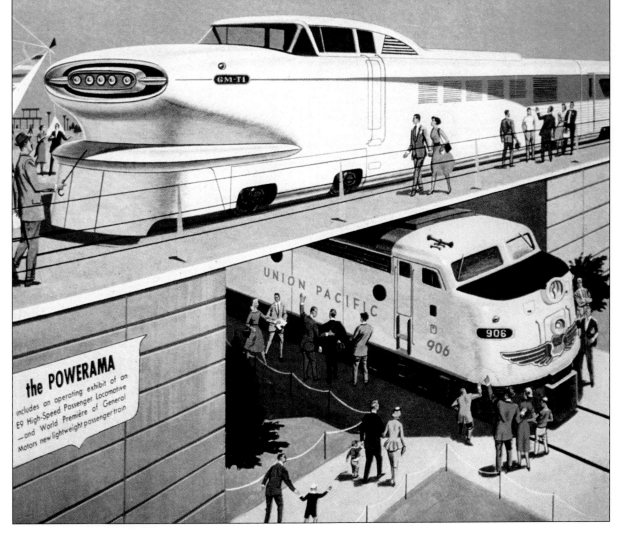

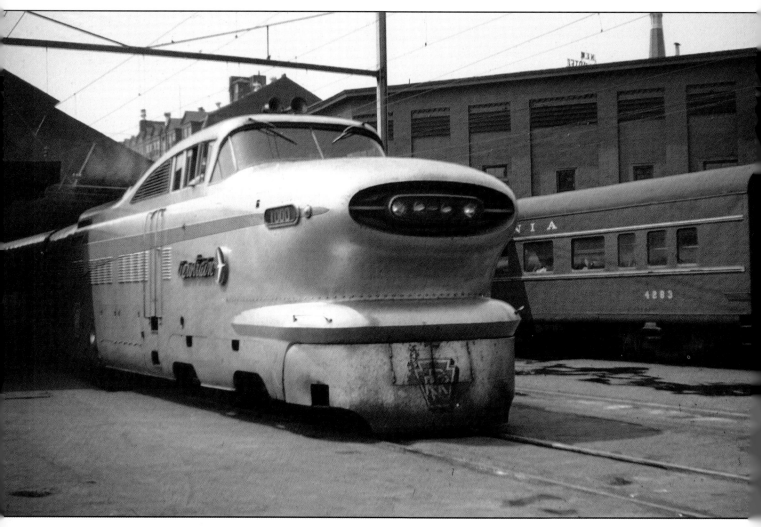

Pennsylvania's *Aerotrain* is seen leaving Harrisburg for Pittsburgh in April 1956. The silver train was in stark contrast to the Tuscan red of Pennsylvania's conventional fleet of passenger cars.

The General Motors "GM" was removed from the observation car on the Pennsylvania's *Aerotrain*, perhaps so as to not conflict with the railroad's keystone. The coupler, air hose and markers appear to be out of place on the futuristic train.

The *Aerotrain* approaches its stop at Niles, Michigan in a nice overhead view in April 1956.

"Dropping Obsolete Services"

From NYC 1957 Annual Report

Safeguarding the financial health of the entire New York Central System and its ability to serve all of its customers demands the discontinuance of obsolete services which drain strength of the system rather than contribute to its well-being. This is especially true of some of our passenger train service, and despite regulatory control of our actions in this field, we were able in 1957 to eliminate more than three million unprofitable passenger train miles.

Our long-term program to abandon unprofitable branch lines continues. In 1957 we obtained public authority to abandon approximately 94 miles of noncompensatory lines with resultant annual savings of about $260,000. The facilities sold or salvaged yielded $3.4 million. Authority was also obtained to discontinue the Weehawken ferries, which represent an annual loss of approximately $1.67 million. The order, however, was upset by a Federal District Court, and we now have it before the United States Supreme Court on appeal. We also closed 57 freight and passenger stations not required by public convenience and necessity. Special trains and extra sections of regular trains were operated only when economically justified. As a result, passenger train miles in 1957 were 10.3% under the previous year.

Northern District trains that had used the Illinois Central Station in Chicago were rerouted to the La Salle Street Station, owned 50% by New York Central, saving rentals and other charges paid to the Illinois Central. We are now seeking permission from state authorities to discontinue all passenger service between Cincinnati and Toledo and between Indianapolis and St. Louis.

Xplorer is seen in Columbus on July 10, 1956. The yellow and blue color scheme was more like that belonging to Chesapeake and Ohio.

Train Design

One of the difficulties of designing railroad equipment is that once in production, it has to complement existing equipment with which it is matched, and once it is in service, the owner (the railroad) has to live with its design for its expected life span. In some cases, this can be from twenty to thirty years.

When the railroads streamlined their trains in the 1930s, a budding (no pun intended) rail car technology would change how the passenger train functioned. Trains were still pulled by steam locomotives which provided heat to the cars in winter, while the cars themselves supplied their own electricity for lights and mechanical air-conditioning.

As the streamlined cars often were intermixed with the "standard" cars then in wide use around the country, and interchanged with other railroads, they had to have systems for steam heat (and electricity, in some cases) which were compatible. In addition, when diesels were placed in service, existing rail car technology dictated the need for steam. Diesels used in passenger service, therefore, had to generate steam through a stream generator which was positioned at the rear of passenger cab engines and in the short hood of road switchers.

By the 1950s, some railroads were experimenting with "headend power"—a design which generated electric power, located either in the engine or a power car, and supplied electricity for heat and lights. This system is used today by Amtrak in the U.S. It was used for the first time on NYC with the *Xplorer*.

A train of the future would have to be completely redesigned. It would have to complement a concept and fit the service it would be expected to provide.

In short, the existing rail car technology of 1950 was outmoded—even obsolete, Young exclaimed—for the era of the second half of the 20th century.

Bibliography

Books

Borkin, Joseph *Robert R. Young, The Populist of Wall Street*. New York: Harper & Row, 1969.

Borntrager, Karl A. *Keeping the Railroads Running*. New York: Hastings House, 1974.

Overton, Richard C. *Burlington Route*. Lincoln, Nebraska: University of Nebraska Press, 1976.

Stover, John F., *The Life and Decline of the American Railroad*. New York: Oxford University Press, 1970.

Swanberg, J. W. *New Haven Power*. Medina, Ohio: Alvin F. Stover, 1988.

Periodicals

Railway Age 1950-1957

Trains Magazine. August 1948 - December 1958.

Corporate Publications

Tracks. 1946-1954. Chesapeake and Ohio Railway.

Future of the Pullman Company. August 1951.
   Robert Heller & Associates.

Report on the Ohio Xplorer. February 1957.
   New York Central Railroad.

What Manner of Man is Robert R. Young? April 1954.
   New York Central Railroad.

The Carbuilder. November 1952.
   Pullman-Standard Car Manufacturing Company.

"Preliminary Information Train X."
   Pullman-Standard Car Manufacturing Company.

"Passengers and Profits."
   Railway Progress Institute: Chicago, 1959.

About the Author

Geoffrey H. Doughty grew up in Winnetka, Illinois watching the 400s of the Chicago and North Western Railway. His association and interest in the New York Central began when his parents took him and his brother east to visit their grandparents each summer. As a student at Franklin College of Indiana, he worked summers for the C&NW as a relief agent in both freight and passenger territory. After graduating from college with a bachelor's degree in history, he taught for two years before going to Maine Central Railroad in the operating department. He was appointed to the safety department in 1982 and was its director when he left the railroad in 1987 to become a safety consultant.

A devotee of classical music, he produces and announces the radio broadcasts of the Portland Symphony Orchestra. He also collects rare recordings.

He and his wife Pamela, live in southern Maine with their two Labrador retrievers. This is his third book about New York Central passenger train operations.

Footnotes

1   Joseph Borkin, Robert R. Young, Populist of Wall Street, p. 1.
2   Robert Heller & Associates, Future of the Pullman Company, p. 1.
3   Ibid, pp. 6-7.
4   Richard Overton, Burlington Route, p. 308.
5   Ibid.
6   Ibid., p. 315.
7   Ibid.
8   John F. Stover, Life and Decline of American Railroads, p.138
9   J. W. Swanberg, New Haven Power, p. 512-513.
10 NYC, What manner of man is Robert R. Young?, p.1.
11 John H. White, Jr., The American Railroad Passenger Car, p. 264.
12 Joseph Borkin, Robert R. Young, Populist of Wall Street, pp. 70-72.
13 U.S. v. Pullman Company, et al., Civil Action No. 994,
      U.S. District of Pennsylvania, pp. 11-12.
14 Joseph Borkin, Robert R. Young, Populist of Wall Street, pp. 74-77.
15 Ibid pp. 81-86.
16 Ibid., p. 98.
17 Tracks, April 1947, p. 3
18 Ibid., p. 4
19 Railway Progress Institute Report, "Passengers and Profits," p. 58.
20 TRAINS Magazine, August 1948, p. 8.
21 The Carbuilder, November 1952, p. 8.
22 GM documents: General Notes on G.M. Train, 6/14/55.
23 Ibid.
24 Ibid.
25 Ibid..
26 Ibid.
27 Ibid.
28 Ibid.
29 Ibid..
30 Karl Borntrager, Keeping the Railroads Running, p. 196.
31 Joseph Borkin, Robert R. Young, Populist of Wall Street, p. 217.
32 Railway Age, November 26, 1956, p. 17.
33 Railway Age, July 4, 1955, p. 11.
34 ibid.
35 Pullman-Standard Manufacturing Company Report,
      "Preliminary Information Train X." p 3.
36 NYC: Report on the Ohio Xplorer, p.4.
37 Ibid., p. 36
38 Ibid, p. 11.
39 Conversation with "Brownie" Markley.
40 Conversation with John S. Gallagher, Jr.
41 Conversation with "Brownie" Markley.
42 Conversation with John S. Gallagher, Jr.
43 "Passengers and Profits," p. 49.
44 Ibid, p. 56.
45 Ibid.
46 Ibid. p. 38.
47 Ibid. p. 59.
48 Ibid.
49 Ibid, p. 60.
50 Borntrager, Karl A., "Keeping the Railroads Running," p. 199.